TV Sets

Fantasy Blueprints
of Classic TV Homes

TV Sets

Fantasy Blueprints
of Classic TV Homes

MARK BENNETT

ROGERS MEMORIAL LIBRARY

TV BOOKS

Keeping books in the picture. ™

TV Books
New York

Copyright © 1996 by TV Books, Inc.
All rights reserved.

Transparencies of the blueprints were photographed by Paula Goldman.
Book and cover design and production by Joe Gannon.

Printed and bound in the United States of America.

ISBN: 1-57500-017-2

CIP data available.

   2   3   4   5   6   7   8   9   10

TV Books publishes books developed from quality television. The company is founded on the principle that books naturally extend the excitement, enjoyment, and entertainment benefits inherent in television.

TV Books, Inc.
Distributed by Penguin USA.

TV Books titles are available at special discounts for bulk purchases for sales promotions, premiums, fund raising or educational use. For details contact:

Special Sales Director
TV Books, Inc.
61 Van Dam Street
New York, NY 10013
http:\\www.tvbooks.com

To Wally Cleaver

Acknowledgements

This book could never have happened without the love and support from the following people: to the staff at TV Books, Ian Cuthbertson, Sommer Hixson, Peter Kaufman, Nina Nowak, I thank you for creating such a beautiful book.

To my parents, Ed & Geneva, my brother, Mike, my sister Gina. To Melody McKenzie-Wood, Dr. Jane Wick, John Morris, Gil Gold, Mathew Gracie, Bert Elias, Suzanne Allen, Dr. Jim Collins, Roger Howard, Michael Hect, and Jonathan Scharer.

To the Mark Moore Gallery, I have been blessed. Thank you, Mark Moore, Eric Mellencamp, Cliff Benjamine, and to Christopher Ford, who recognized my work and took a chance on me.

—M. B.
Santa Monica

Table of Contents

Foreword

I stumbled—quite accidentally—onto Mark Bennett's blueprints *en masse* in the bar of a Silverlake restaurant in Los Angeles in August 1995.

It wasn't until I was standing at the bar, waiting for the drinks I had ordered for myself and friends, that my eye lingered on one of these blueprints, and as I focused on it the name Mary Richards penetrated my brain.

"What the. . . ," I said, " I *KNOW* Mary Richards!"

Suddenly these mechanical, cold, and blue images were gushing warmth, love, and happiness (I had had *one* drink).

All these shows had left a profound mark on my childhood (whether one watched all of them or not was not as important as which ones you watched *OVER* others). These literal imprints both confirmed that another had shared my affliction, was recovering into adulthood (only adults can be nostalgic—right???), and reminded me at the same time of my own marginalization—as the TV lives I treasured as a child were the lives I would never replicate.

These were Valentines, certainly—but from a pining and enduring love, or from a bittersweet tragic breakup?

"I think I better call this guy. . ."

—Christopher Ford,
Mark Moore Gallery

Preface

First off, I created these drawings over a 20-year period because 1) I wanted to, in some way, capture all the details of these television families, and 2) I figured if I could geographically, architecturally and chronologically record these imaginary houses and their inhabitants, then I would become part of these television families and they would become part of me.

I began with small sketches, sometimes on the back of envelopes or a receipt or simple scratch paper. Being that most of these drawings were done in an era before the VCR, they had to be done quickly while my imagination was still in overdrive. When I felt I had a substantial amount of information and thinking together, I would do a formal drawing on architectural paper, with border line and title block, and then run to the blueprint shop for an official print. While my collection of drawings grew, I began to fantasize about building a utopian neighborhood, where instead of a Spanish villa or a ranch house, you could choose a Mike & Carol Brady or a Darrin & Samantha Stevens to live in.

These drawings were my own very personal joy, and were hidden for years under my bed. It wasn't until after I got up the nerve to exhibit them (in a bar in Hollywood) that I finally released them for others to see. Now, I don't know if a utopian TV neighborhood is such a good idea. I mean, what if you built a Mike & Carol Brady house and then didn't have enough children to fill it up? Or, if you chose Mary Richards's apartment, does that mean you have to drive . . . a Ford Mustang?

Being human, I realize that there are less than perfect details in these imaginary blueprints. The sets did change, and story lines changed so that crews would alter the sets. But in general, I tried to make these houses complete (with bathrooms, which were rarely shown) and buildable. I didn't draw them for fame or fortune. I drew them for love.

—M. B.
Santa Monica
August 1996

Ward & June Cleaver's Grant Avenue House

The Cleavers' first house at 513 Grant Avenue is a wood-sided, two-story structure with a detached one-car garage. It is painted a light color with dark trim. The entrance has a covered porch with distinctive wood-slat benches for sitting and a top-flap mailbox to the left of the front door. The front yard is completely enclosed by a picket fence—a perfect place for Ward to teach Beaver tumbling.

Inside, off the foyer, a staircase with railing ascends to the second level. To the left is a living room, with a fireplace and mantle painted white, bookshelves. a window seat, a desk with a phone, and two easy chairs. Beyond the living room, at the front of the house, is a den, which is never shown.

A pair of French doors open to a patio at the rear of the living room, beyond the set of built-in couches and an archway, with columns and glass-faced bookshelves. There is a sedate dining room with seating for six. A potted philodendron rests on top of a single credenza near the sheer-curtained windows.

To the right of the foyer, through a double swinging door, is a cozy kitchen, with breakfast area consisting of an Early American table and chairs with a matching china hutch. A self-contained stove with a decorative ventilation hood stands next to the refrigerator. Sink and cabinets with tile countertops show off an impeccably clean work space. Glass-faced cupboards display June's china—complete sets, no chips. Beaver often uses the cutting board as a stepladder to help put away the dinner plates. A windowed service door near the breakfast table opens to a service porch (for milk delivery), two trash bins and the garage, where Ward stows his Ford Fairlane, as well as a set of power tools and wood-working equipment extensive enough to build a go-cart for Wally and the Beav.

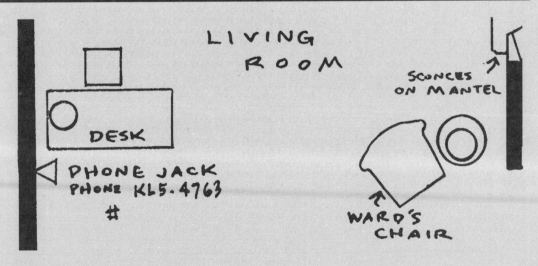

LIVING ROOM

DESK

PHONE JACK
PHONE KL5-4763
#

SCONCES ON MANTEL

WARD'S CHAIR

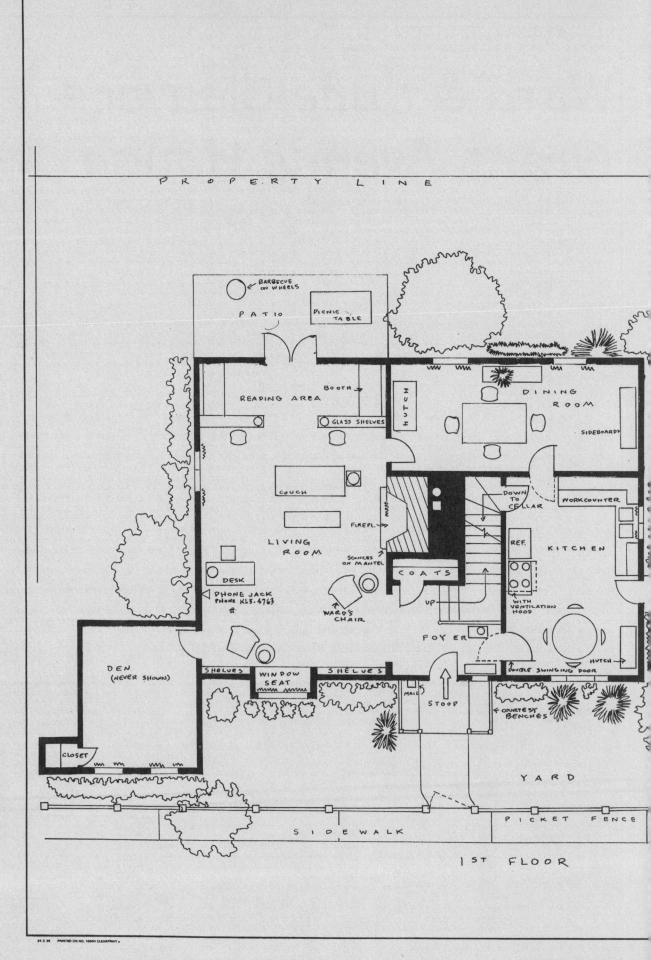

PROPERTY LINE

BARBECUE ON WHEELS

PATIO

PICNIC TABLE

READING AREA

BOOTH

HUTCH

DINING ROOM

GLASS SHELVES

SIDEBOARD

COUCH

DOWN TO CELLAR

WORKCOUNTER

FIREPL.

REF.

KITCHEN

LIVING ROOM

SCONCES ON MANTEL

COATS

DESK

PHONE JACK
PHONE KL5-4763
#

WARD'S CHAIR

UP

WITH VENTILATION HOOD

FOYER

HUTCH

DEN
(NEVER SHOWN)

SHELVES

WINDOW SEAT

SHELVES

MAIL

STOOP

DOUBLE SWINGING DOOR

COURTESY BENCHES

CLOSET

YARD

SIDEWALK

PICKET FENCE

1ST FLOOR

2

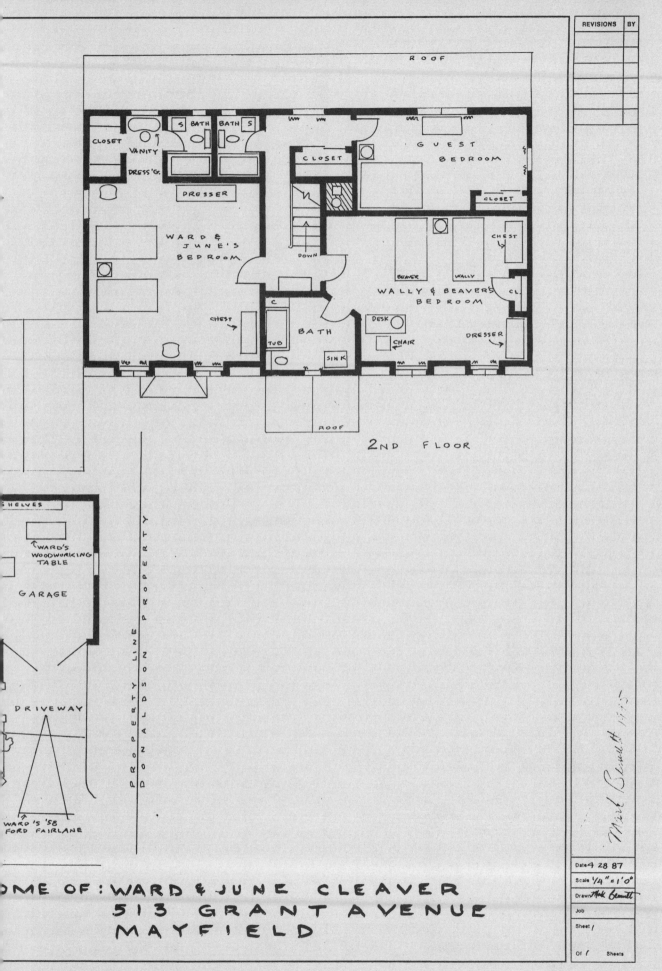

ROOF

CLOSET

S BATH | BATH S

VANITY

DRESS'G.

DRESSER

CLOSET

GUEST BEDROOM

CLOSET

WARD & JUNE'S BEDROOM

DOWN

CHEST

BEAVER

WALLY

CHEST

WALLY & BEAVERS BEDROOM

CL.

CHEST

C

DESK

CHAIR

DRESSER

TUB

BATH

SINK

ROOF

2ND FLOOR

SHELVES

WARD'S WOODWORKING TABLE

GARAGE

PROPERTY LINE   DONALDSON PROPERTY

DRIVEWAY

WARD'S '58 FORD FAIRLANE

OME OF: WARD & JUNE CLEAVER
513 GRANT AVENUE
MAYFIELD

Date 4 28 87
Scale 1/4" = 1'0"
Drawn Mark Bennett
Job
Sheet 1
Of 1   Sheets

"LEAVE IT TO BEAVER"

3

Running under the main staircase, via a doorway in the kitchen, is a cellar where a washer and dryer are located, alongside a wicker laundry basket. The basement is damp and a perfect spot for Wally and Beaver to raise their mail-order alligator.

Upstairs, there are two bathrooms, a guest room, Ward and June's bedroom, and the boys' room. Wally and Beaver's room features twin beds and a dresser with a mirror. Nautical touches abound here. It's a pleasant room with little clutter—but don't check the closets. The boys share a tiled bath with tub and matching sink. This bathroom (above the foyer) has a window overlooking the yard. This window is easy to open, as attested by a four-year-old girl named Puddin', who crawled out on the roof during a Saturday afternoon babysitting stint. Neither the boys nor the house will ever be the same.

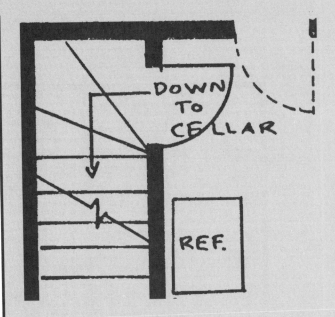

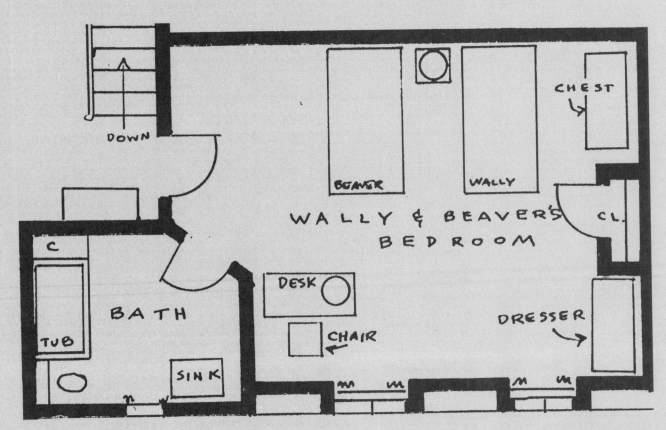

Ward & June Cleaver's Pine Street House

Ward and June Cleaver's house at 211 Pine Street in Mayfield was a step up for them. Ward, after all, has got to be doing pretty well as an accountant.

With plenty of flagstone on the ground floor, the Cleaver home exudes warmth and sophistication. Ward's book-lined den to the left of the foyer, and spacious living room to the right, make for a great entertaining spot, like for Wally's teen parties, or when Beaver invites Miss Landers, his teacher, for dinner. Beyond the living room, shuttered doors open onto a formal dining room with French doors leading out to a flagstone terrace with a redwood picnic table.

June's kitchen is a marvel of convenience, like her built-in double ovens, island range counter and refrigerator with freezer compartment below. A wall phone is mounted to the wall by the service door, and a laundry room is just beyond the kitchen sink counter.

A breezeway, with bougainvillea trellis, extends from the service porch to the garage where Ward parks his nearly new Plymouth automobile. Behind the garage is a woodbox, a great place for firewood. A large, level backyard features a mature oak tree.

Upstairs, Wally and Beaver share a bedroom, this time with a large bathroom and the same nautical-themed wood furniture. Ward and June's bedroom also has its own bathroom and a television (on wheels) for late-night viewing. There is room for separate guests to visit, like Aunt Martha and Uncle Billy. A large linen closet is prominent at the top of the stairs.

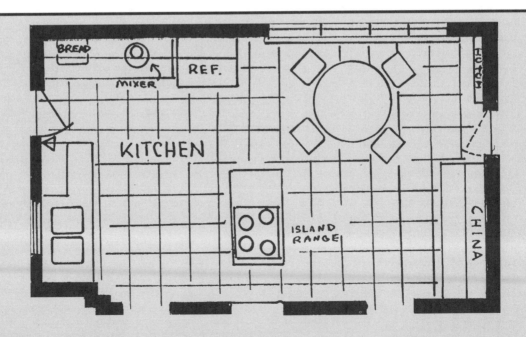

PROPERTY LINE

WALKWAY

FLOWER BED

TE

DINING

WOOD BOX

WOODWORKING

SERVICE

BREA

MIXER

REF.

HUTCH

KITCHEN

CHINA

GARAGE

ISLAND RANGE

W.H.

DOUBLE OVENS

LINEN

PANTRY

LAUNDRY

LAV.

STORAGE

FIREPLACE

DRYER

WASHER

S

SINK

COATS

LIVING

SHELVES

SHELVES

SHELVES

UP

T.V.

WARD'S DEN

FOYER

DRIVEWAY

TRELLIS

MAIL

ROOF

UP

HOME OF: WARD &
211 PINE
MAYFI

6

34 X 36   PRINTED ON NO. 1000H CLEARPRINT ®

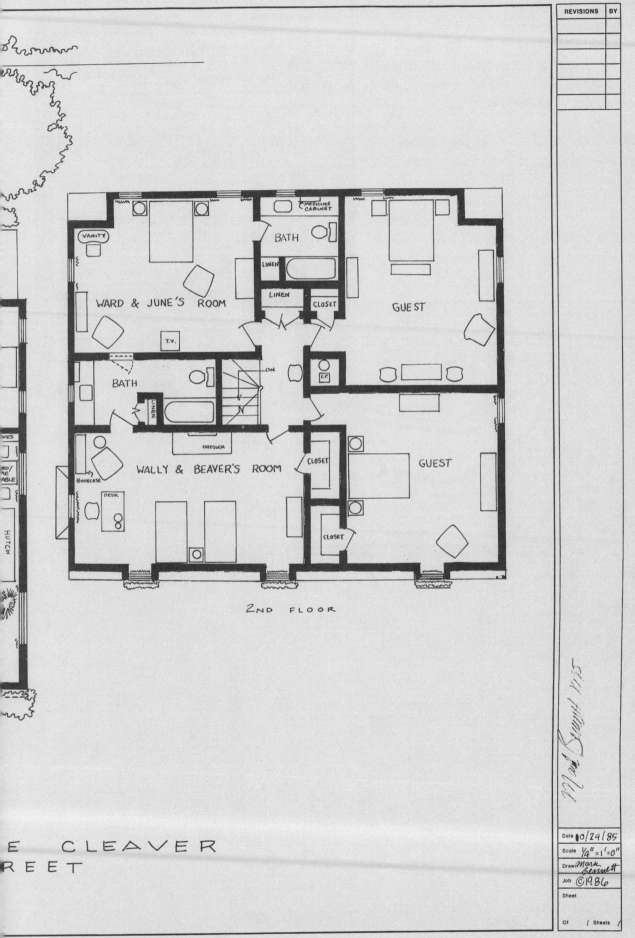

WARD & JUNE'S ROOM

VANITY

BATH

MEDICINE CABINET

LINEN

LINEN

CLOSET

GUEST

T.V.

BATH

LINEN

DN.

E.R.

DRESSER

WALLY & BEAVER'S ROOM

CLOSET

GUEST

BOOKCASE

DESK

CLOSET

2ND FLOOR

E CLEAVER
REET

HUTCH

"LEAVE IT TO BEAVER"

Date 10/29/85
Scale ¼" = 1'=0"
Draw Mark Bennett
Job ©1986
Sheet
Of / Sheets

A nicely decorated house, it is. Ward and June should be proud of the personal touches like the framed pictures of Pinkie and Blue Boy in the foyer or the waist-high world globe in the bay window in Ward's den. And even when Beaver leaves the water running in the upstairs bathtub (which ruins the kitchen ceiling below), the Cleavers keep their home in immaculate condition. Why, any father who forces his son to sell his first car because it clutters up the driveway and makes the neighborhood look less than serene is a wonderful neighbor indeed. No wonder there are never any "for sale" signs on Pine Avenue.

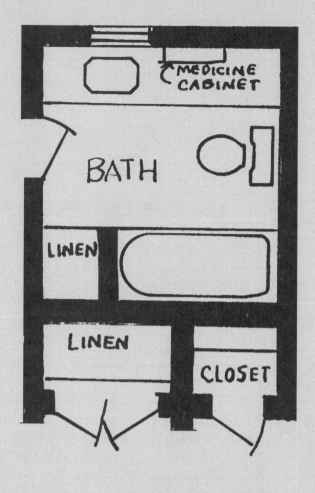

MEDICINE CABINET

BATH

LINEN

LINEN

CLOSET

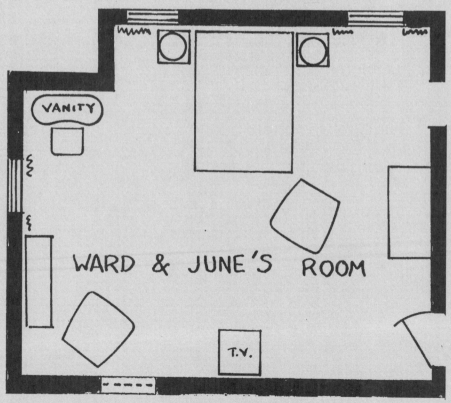

VANITY

WARD & JUNE'S ROOM

T.V.

"FATHER KNOWS BEST"

Jim & Margaret Anderson House

Jim Anderson bought the house at 607 Maple Street for his wife Margaret and their three children, Betty (Princess), Bud (Jim, Jr.) and Cathy (Kitten). The house, a quaint Dutch Colonial, has a wood shingle roof with three gables and spans almost 4,000 feet of living space on two levels.

The Anderson home features a den, a formal dining room (with kitchen pass-through), a bay-windowed breakfast nook, a built-in outdoor brick barbecue, a trash incinerator, a service porch, and a detached two-car garage. Bought in 1945 while Jim was still a struggling insurance agent, the Anderson home was secured with a loan from the Bank of Springfield and financed through the G.I. Bill for a first-time home-buyer. As all families at this time have a limited budget, the Anderson home remains modestly furnished, yet warm and inviting.

Margaret favors Early American furniture, bought on time plan from the better stores in town, a conservative arrangement of maple and chintz, cane-seated dining chairs, a china hutch, even a Windsor bench in the foyer. Built-in bookcases flank either side of the living-room entrance, their shelves lined with volumes of Robert Frost and a dog-eared copy of Silas Marner.

Jim always buys Ford sedans, kept in the manually-opening garage. Besides an occasional hunting or fishing trip with his buddies, he really enjoys the solitude of his den, a cozy room located off the foyer. Although Jim, on more than one occasion, complains that he needs some peace and quiet, as he has brought work home from the office, the smile on his face tells anyone he secretly enjoys his work for the General Insurance Company. The den features a desk, desk chair, and a comfortable couch under the window with end tables on either side, a choice room for hibernating or having a heart-to-heart with everyone's favorite Dad.

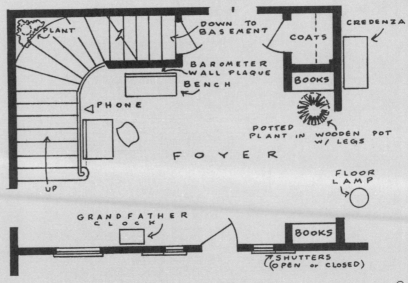

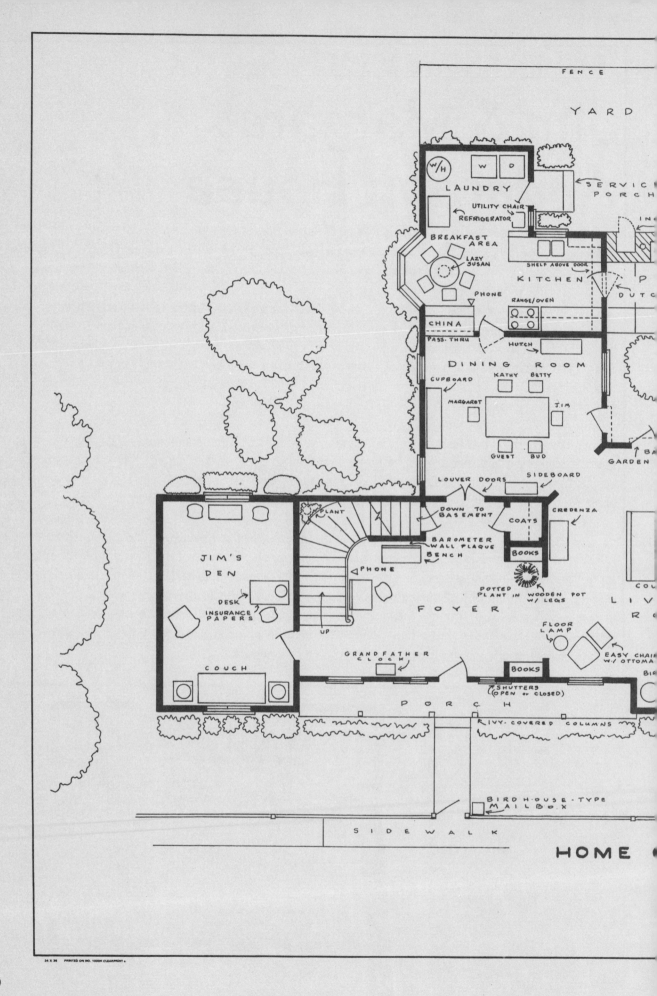

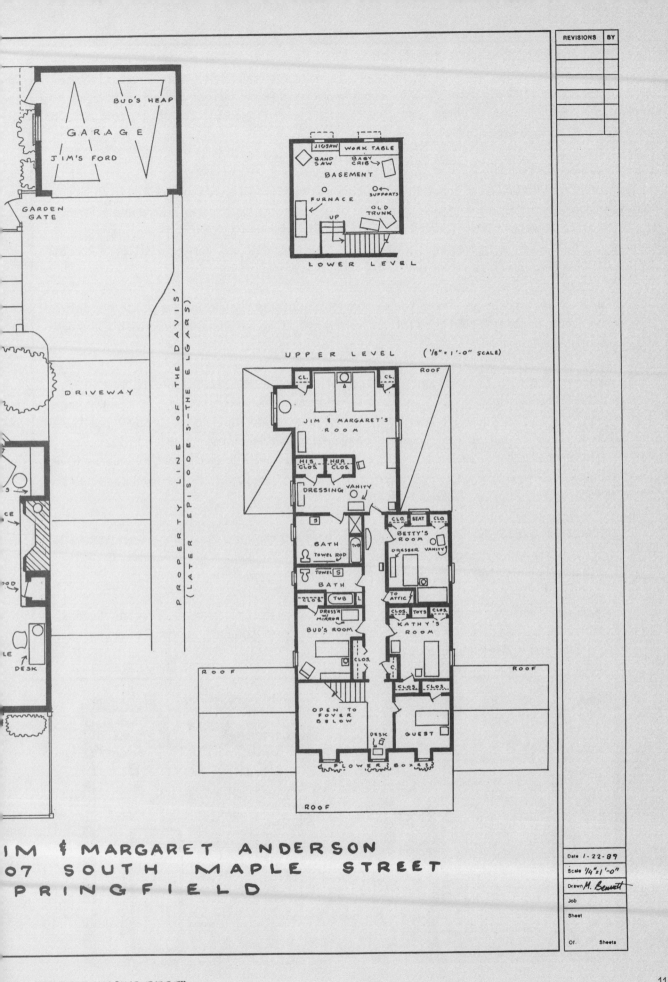

GARAGE

BUD'S HEAP

JIM'S FORD

GARDEN GATE

DRIVEWAY

PROPERTY LINE OF THE DAVIS'
(LATER EPISODE 5—THE ELGARS)

DESK

LOWER LEVEL

JIGSAW   WORK TABLE
BAND SAW   BABY CRIB
BASEMENT
FURNACE   SUPPORTS
UP   OLD TRUNK

UPPER LEVEL   (⅛" = 1'-0" SCALE)

ROOF

CL.   CL.

JIM & MARGARET'S ROOM

HIS CLOS.   HER CLOS.

DRESSING   VANITY

S

BATH   TV

TOWEL ROD

TOWEL S

BATH

CLOS.   TUB

DRESS'N MIRROR

BUD'S ROOM

CLOS.

CLO.   SEAT   CLO.

BETTY'S ROOM

DRESSER   VANITY

TO ATTIC

CLOS.   TOYS   CLOS.

KATHY'S ROOM

C.

ROOF

ROOF

CLO.   CLOS.

OPEN TO FOYER BELOW

DESK   GUEST

FLOWER BOXES

ROOF

IM & MARGARET ANDERSON
07 SOUTH MAPLE STREET
PRINGFIELD

Date 1-22-89
Scale ¼"=1'-0"
Drawn M. Bennett
Job
Sheet
Of.   Sheets

"FATHER KNOWS BEST"

11

The living room consists of a fluffy couch, a bird cage, a game table, another desk with chair, and an inviting wing chair with an ottoman. Bookshelves occupy the corner near a bay-window overlooking an alcove garden accessible through a single French door. A woodbox holds an ample supply of kindling for the fireplace. Louver doors can be closed to shut off the formal dining room—a central place for entertaining.

Via a double swinging kitchen door, one must pass through the dining room to arrive at this glistening linoleum-floored work space with an unobstructed view of the laundry room from the breakfast nook, a round table carved into a niche of yet another bay window. There is a washer and dryer and hot-water heater (that leaked so bad, Jim once had to cancel a camping trip). There is a fully-stocked refrigerator, full of healthy snacks like custard cups and leftovers in neatly wrapped tin foil, placed near a family-size jar of real mayonnaise.

The built-in barbecue grill faces the service porch outside the distinctive Dutch door off the kitchen, while the incinerator (used for leaf-raking refuse) faces the back yard with a laundry-room entrance.

Upstairs, there are five bedrooms and two bathrooms. Bud's room is the smallest. Kathy's room features a built-in toy chest and two closets. Betty's room has a built-in window seat, a great place to contemplate the theme for the next school dance or to cry over lost love. She also has twin beds, set up in a corner of the room, an excellent arrangement for sleepovers and all-night girl talk. Jim and Margaret's room, arranged at the end of the hall, has his-and-hers closets amidst cabbage-rose wallpaper. There are matching bedspreads on the twin beds and an adjoining bath is near Margaret's dressing table.

An attic staircase off the upstairs hallway affords a treasure trove of old college pennants, badminton racquets and a musty raccoon coat. It's a perfect place for playing dress-up or for going down Memory Lane. Need a flapper outfit? You'll find it here.

In the basement, via a stairwell under the main stairs in the foyer, you'll find the furnace, old picture frames and a collection of baby furniture. But don't look for the crib. The Andersons gave it to a young expectant couple in need.

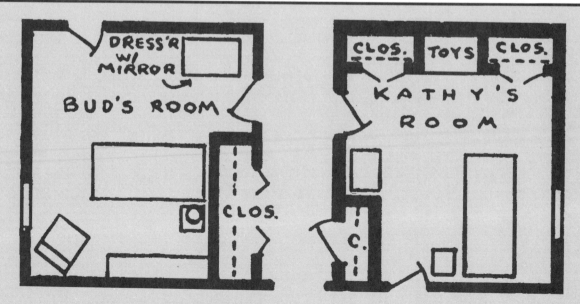

Dr. Alex & Donna Stone House

Hilldale is the setting for the home of Donna and Alex Stone. Nestled in a quiet neighborhood, these homes, with their picture-perfect shrubs and freshly-painted gables, are doubtless the icons of style and good breeding for their town.

The Stone house is a sedate Colonial, with three dormer windows upstairs and a large porch extending beyond the entranceway. Entering the house, you've got a prominent staircase separating the living room from the foyer. A telephone table and chair stand at the base of the stairs.

The living-room and dining-room are handsomely appointed—comfortable but not snooty. The kitchen, beyond the staircase, and accessible from the foyer, is mighty efficient—with an island range-top, built-in refrigerator, a sparkling-clean oven and an intimate breakfast nook.

Dr. Stone's physician's office, to the right of the front door, is approached through a pair of louvered doors. This is his examining room, for a while, until his practice picks up. There are medical books, examining tools, medicines. A lavatory is accessible from this room. Golf clubs are stored in

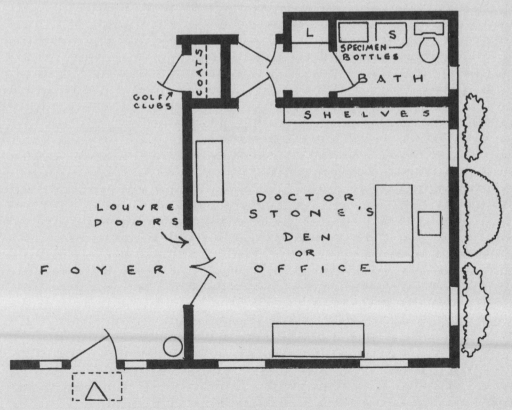

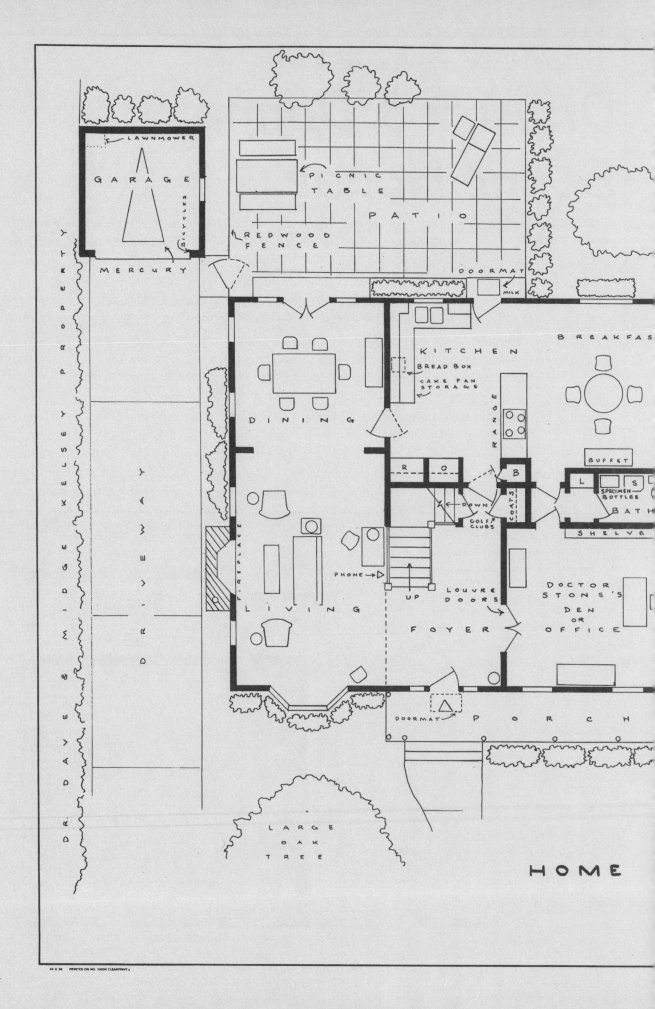

LAWNMOWER

G A R A G E

Bicycles

M E R C U R Y

PICNIC TABLE

P A T I O

REDWOOD FENCE

DOORMAT

MILK

B R E A K F A S

KITCHEN

BREAD BOX

CAKE PAN STORAGE

RANGE

BUFFET

R O O

B

L S

COATS

SPECIMEN BOTTLES

B A T H

DOWN

GOLF CLUBS

SHELVE

D I N I N G

FIREPLACE

DOWN

PHONE

UP

LOUVRE DOORS

DOCTOR STONE'S DEN OR OFFICE

L I V I N G

F O Y E R

DOORMAT

P O R C H

DR. DAVE & MIDGE KELSEY PROPERTY

D R I V E W A Y

L A R G E O A K T R E E

H O M E

24 X 36   PRINTED ON NO. 1000H CLEARPRINT

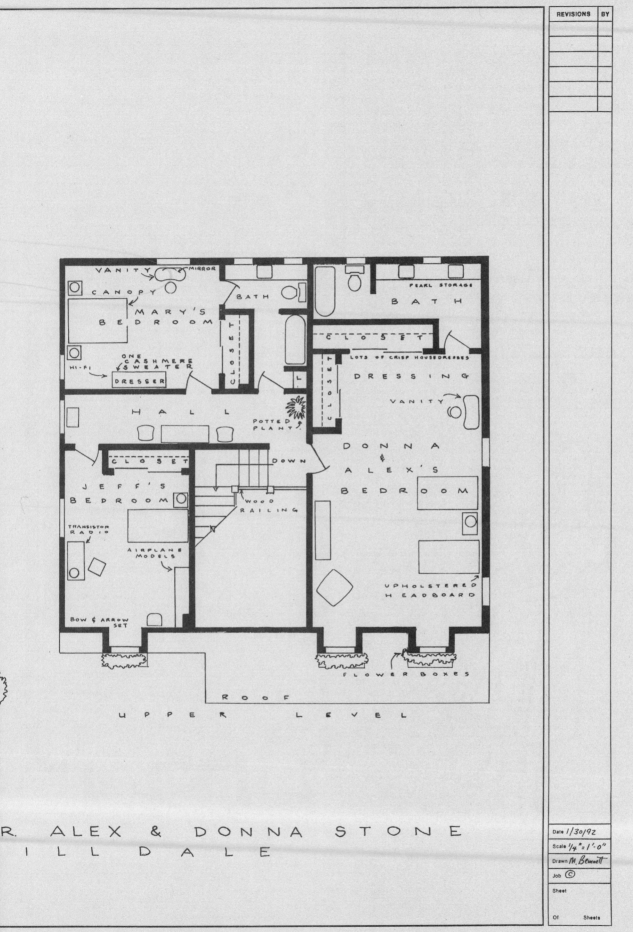

VANITY MIRROR

CANOPY

MARY'S BEDROOM

BATH

HI-FI

ONE CASHMERE SWEATER

DRESSER

CLOSET

PEARL STORAGE

BATH

CLOSET

LOTS OF CRISP HOUSEDRESSES

DRESSING

VANITY

CLOSET

HALL

POTTED PLANT

DOWN

DONNA & ALEX'S BEDROOM

CLOSET

JEFF'S BEDROOM

WOOD RAILING

TRANSISTOR RADIO

AIRPLANE MODELS

BOW & ARROW SET

UPHOLSTERED HEADBOARD

FLOWER BOXES

ROOF

UPPER LEVEL

R. ALEX & DONNA STONE
ILLDALE

"THE DONNA REED SHOW"

REVISIONS | BY

Date 1/30/92
Scale 1/4"=1'-0"
Drawn M. Bennett
Job ©
Sheet
Of   Sheets

the hall closet and Mercury automobiles fill the double detached garage off the wood-fenced patio out back.

Upstairs, there are three bedrooms, the master suite being the largest, with a private bath and two closets. His-and-her twin beds complete the picture, with a handy Princess phone for emergency late-night doctor calls.

Jeff and Mary each have their own room, decorated in their own individual tastes. They share a bath down the hall.

This house is where the neighborhood kids gather, an inviting home with a fully-stocked refrigerator and seven-layer cake fresh from the oven.

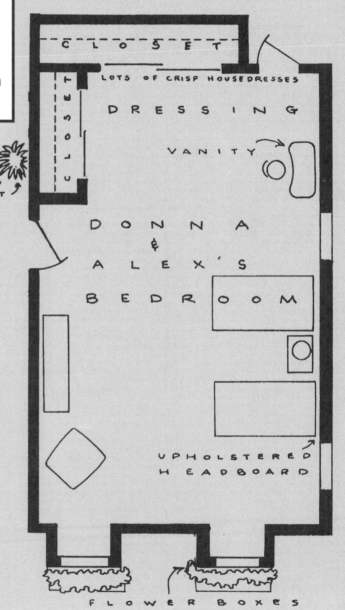

POTTED PLANT

CLOSET

CLOSET

LOTS OF CRISP HOUSEDRESSES

DRESSING

VANITY

DONNA & ALEX'S BEDROOM

UPHOLSTERED HEADBOARD

FLOWER BOXES

"THE DONNA REED SHOW"

Home of Martin & Natalie Lane

At number eight Remsen, in the comfortable Brooklyn Heights area of New York City, is the home of Martin and Natalie Lane and their children, Ross and Patty, and visiting cousin, Cathy. A regal brownstone, the Lane home features high ceilings, a large reception foyer with cloak room, and an inviting living room with cozy fireplace and built-in window seat. There is a baby grand piano in the corner. No doubt this is a fitting environment for the senior editor of the New York-based *Chronicle* newspaper and his lovely wife.

A full-service kitchen is in pristine order thanks to the dedication of the housekeeper, Mrs. McDonald.

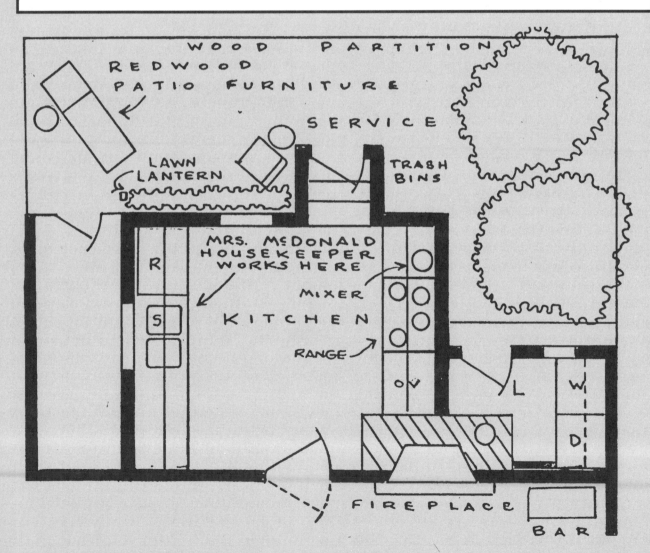

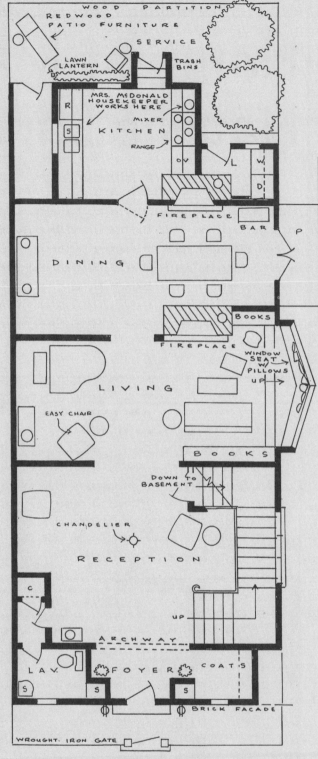

WOOD PARTITION

REDWOOD
PATIO FURNITURE

SERVICE

LAWN
LANTERN

TRASH
BINS

R

MRS. McDONALD
HOUSEKEEPER
WORKS HERE

MIXER

KITCHEN

S

RANGE

OV

L W

D

FIREPLACE

BAR

P

DINING

BOOKS

FIREPLACE

WINDOW
SEAT
W/
PILLOWS
UP

LIVING

EASY CHAIR

BOOKS

DOWN TO
BASEMENT

UP

CHANDELIER

RECEPTION

C

UP

ARCHWAY

LAV.

FOYER

COATS

S

S

S

BRICK FACADE

WROUGHT IRON GATE

HOME

⇐ TO SNACK SHOP

⇓ TO SUBWAY & MANHATTAN

SPECIFICATIONS

SPEC 1) ALL CEILINGS 14 FT. HIGH

2) ADDED ELECTRICAL OUTLETS
& WATTAGE IN DAUGHTER'S
BEDROOM FOR HAIRDRYERS

3) EXTRA PHONE JACKS IN
DAUGHTER'S BEDROOM

18

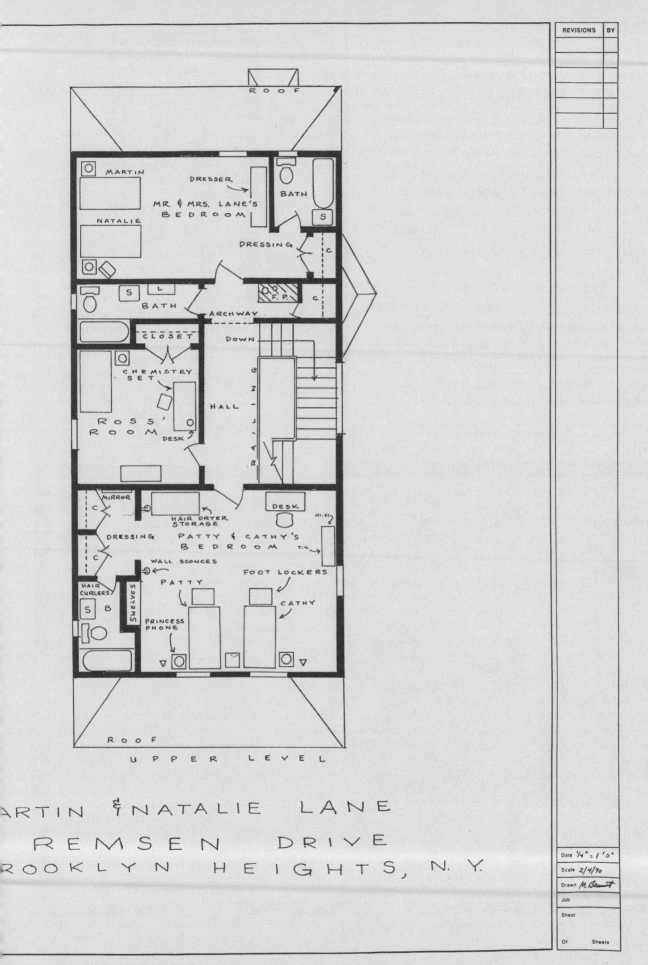

ROOF

MARTIN

NATALIE

DRESSER

MR. & MRS. LANE'S
BEDROOM

BATH

S

DRESSING

C

BATH

S   L

ARCHWAY

F.P.

C

CLOSET

DOWN

CHEMISTRY
SET

ROSS'
ROOM

HALL

G
O
I
N
G

D
O
W
N

DESK

MIRROR

C

DESK

HI-FI

HAIR DRYER
STORAGE

DRESSING

PATTY & CATHY'S
BEDROOM

T.V.

C

WALL SCONCES

FOOT LOCKERS

HAIR
CURLERS

S B

SHELVES

PATTY

PRINCESS
PHONE

CATHY

ROOF

U P P E R   L E V E L

ARTIN & NATALIE LANE

REMSEN   DRIVE

ROOKLYN   HEIGHTS, N. Y.

REVISIONS   BY

Date ¼" = 1'0"
Scale 2/4/90
Drawn M. Bennett
Job
Sheet
Of   Sheets

Upstairs, via a sweeping staircase, are the three generous bedrooms. Martin and Natalie's room features twin beds, a dressing area, and a private bath. Ross's room is highlighted by an elaborate chemistry set and a collection of trading cards. Patty and Cathy share a bedroom above the parlor floor at the front of the house. There is a separate bath with haircare products galore, footlockers before each twin bed for seasonal wardrobe storage and an extra jack for the constantly ringing Princess telephone.

There are built-in bookshelves, wall sconces, large arched windows, and elaborate crown moldings throughout this home. The Lane home has a brick facade, a wrought-iron entrance gate, and is in close proximity to schools, churches, public transportation, and most importantly, the malt shop.

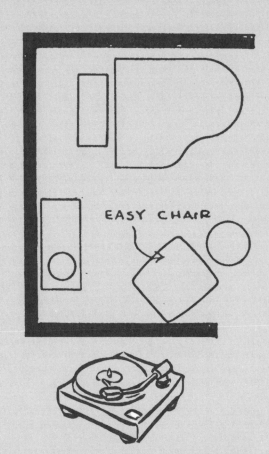

EASY CHAIR

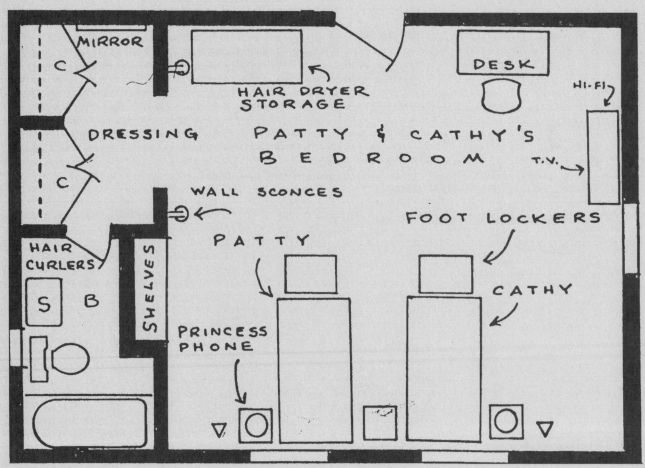

MIRROR

C

C

DRESSING

HAIR DRYER STORAGE

PATTY & CATHY'S BEDROOM

DESK

HI-FI

T.V.

WALL SCONCES

HAIR CURLERS

S B

SHELVES

PATTY

FOOT LOCKERS

CATHY

PRINCESS PHONE

Home of George & Dorothy Baxter

Drive down the winding, sidewalk-lined Marshall Road in Hydeberg, New York, and you can't help but notice the curb appeal of the house at 123. Set back from the street, and situated across from a small park, the Baxter residence has that manicured-lawn look of a garden-society blue-ribbon winner.

Bay windows trimmed in white and bordered in flagstone, a second-story row of windows protruding from a single dormer, an elegant front door in a Dutch Colonial tradition, the Baxter house has style. And the people who live here are stylish, too. Just check out the crisp, heavily starched uniforms on the maid, Hazel.

Enter the foyer with its open staircase (a single potted plant on the landing), check out the cute little telephone table with an olive-green rotary dial phone and the custom-cushioned bay window seat in the living area, and you'll realize that this interior has been created with great flair by part-time decorator (and full-time Mom) Dorothy Baxter.

A hallway under the staircase leads to George's den—a haven for business deals, law books, etc. There is no dust here. Nor in the dining room, with the highly-polished Queen Anne table and seating for six. French doors, ensconced in white sheers, beckon you to step out onto a flagstone terrace, perfect for outdoor tea parties, off the dining room and kitchen. A full-service kitchen with double ovens is complimented by a bay-window breakfast booth in vibrant blue. Maid's quarters, laundry facilities, and Mrs. Baxter's interior decorating studio surround the patio out back.

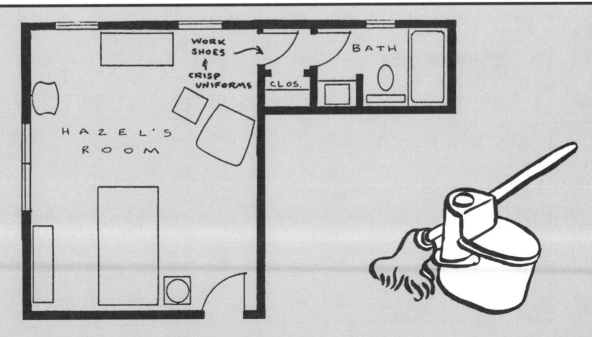

HAZEL'S ROOM

WORK SHOES & CRISP UNIFORMS

CLOS.

BATH

WASHER DRYER

LAUND.

LAV.

LINEN

WORK TABLE

SHELVES

MISSY'S DECORATOR STUDIO

W.H.

SERVICE

DIEDRA HAS SLEPT HERE

REF

WORK TABLE

BAY WINDOW BOOTH

KITCHEN

OVEN

PATIO

GUEST ROOM

BUFFET

DOUBLE-SWINGING DOOR

CHINA

DINING ROOM

FRENCH DOORS

WOOD POLES

FIREPLACE

WOOD

U.P.

SHELVES

GEORGE'S DEN

CLOS.

SERVICE ENTRANCE

BOOKSHELVES BELOW

PHONE

DESK

LAV.

F.P.

LIVING ROOM

FOYER

LAW BOOKS

CURTAINS

FLAGSTONE

MAILBOX

COATS

SHELF

U.P.

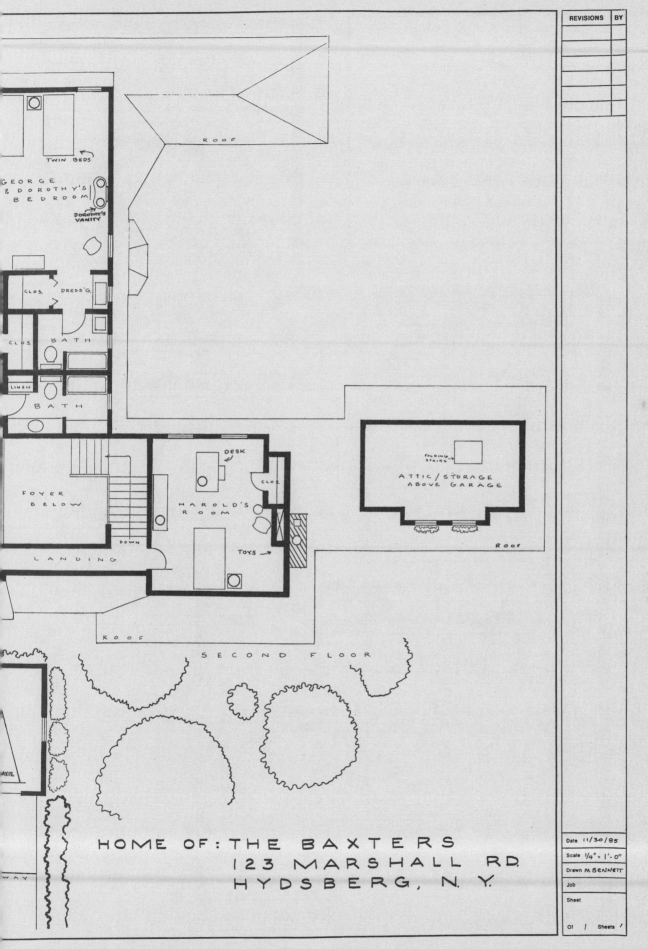

ROOF

TWIN BEDS

GEORGE
& DOROTHY'S
BEDROOM

Dorothy's
VANITY

CLOS. DRESS'G.

CLOS. BATH

LINEN

BATH

DESK

CLOS.

FOYER
BELOW

HAROLD'S
ROOM

DOWN

TOYS →

LANDING

ROOF

FOLDING
STAIRS

ATTIC/STORAGE
ABOVE GARAGE

ROOF

SECOND FLOOR

HOME OF: THE BAXTERS
123 MARSHALL RD,
HYDSBERG, N. Y.

REVISIONS	BY

Date 11/30/85
Scale 1/4" = 1'-0"
Drawn M. BENNETT
Job
Sheet
Of   /   Sheets /

"HAZEL"

Upstairs, there are enough bedrooms for Harold, Dorothy and George—and George's haughty sister, Diedre—for sleepovers.

A double garage, with room above for a guest unit, is attached to the house by a breezeway. The Baxters are a three-car Ford family. A stationwagon for Dorothy, a convertible for Mr B., a Falcon for Hazel. Even Aunt Diedre drives a Thunderbird. Now if we could just lengthen that driveway.

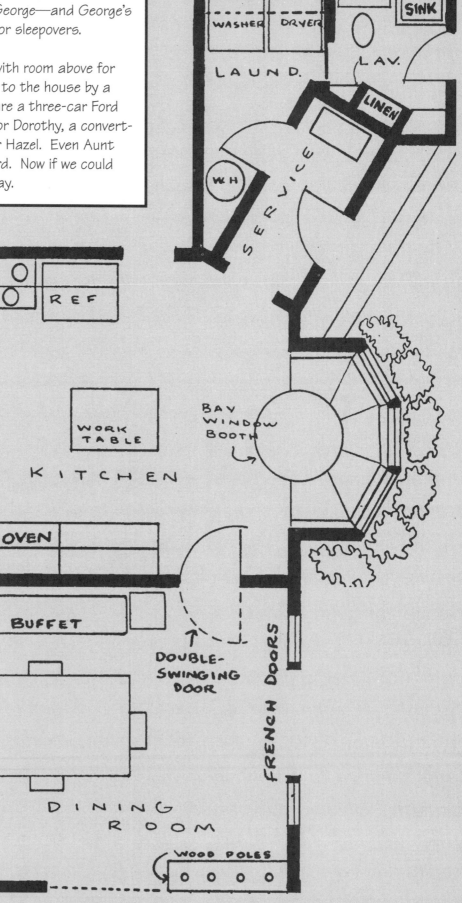

WASHER DRYER SINK
LAUND. LAV.
LINEN
SERVICE
WH

REF
WORK TABLE
KITCHEN
BAY WINDOW BOOTH
OVEN
DOUBLE-SWINGING DOOR
BUFFET
FRENCH DOORS
CHINA
DINING ROOM
WOOD POLES

"HAZEL"

Wilbur & Carol Post House

Wilbur and Carol Post's house at 17230 Valley Road in Los Angeles is a horse-lover's paradise. Living on their half-acre of equestrian-zoned land, the Posts can enjoy the solitude of the country yet maintain their city roots by decorating their architectural abode in high style.

Past a split-rail fence and curved driveway, the visitor observes a quaint Dutch Colonial rancher, with one predominant second-floor gable and a large picture window, nestled in mature shrubbery.

Through a pair of Dutch doors, you step onto a raised slate entryway with a curved staircase to the left, an open sunken living room below. Norman Fox McGregor couch, pedestal tables, a Palos Verdes stone fireplace with cantilevered hearth, café curtains on a seat-cushioned bay window—and you have Don-Loper-in-Big-Bear sophistication in a rustic setting. There is a sliding glass door out to a patio where Wilbur and Carol relax, as well as a combo stables/office where Mr. Ed, the talking horse, resides. Split into a dual barn/architect's studio, Wilbur enjoys all the privacy of this creative oasis just yards from the house. Telephone, television, a daybed/couch, a drawing-board—Wilbur's office is complete.

There is a master suite upstairs with his-and-her closets, and a modern kitchen with glass above and below the wall cupboards on the main floor.

A double carport houses a series of Studebaker automobiles and a top-of-the-line horse trailer. Kay and Roger Addison, and then later the Colonel and his wife, are the chummy neighbors who do not question why Wilbur would tow Mr. Ed on their road trip to Escondido.

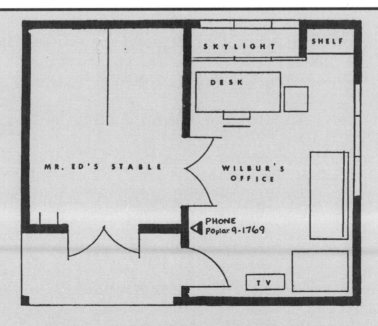

The neighbor-hood has to be fairly tony for the likes of Mae West to move in next door. And when the famed pro-wrestler Ricky Starr stays with the Posts for an extended period, you can be sure the neigh-bors get out their autograph books.

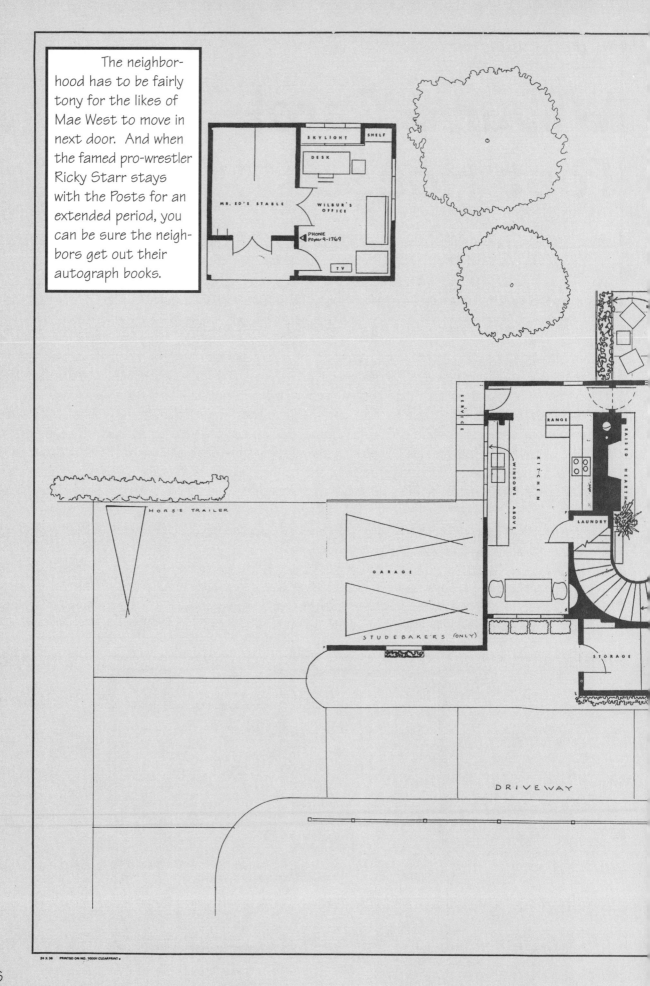

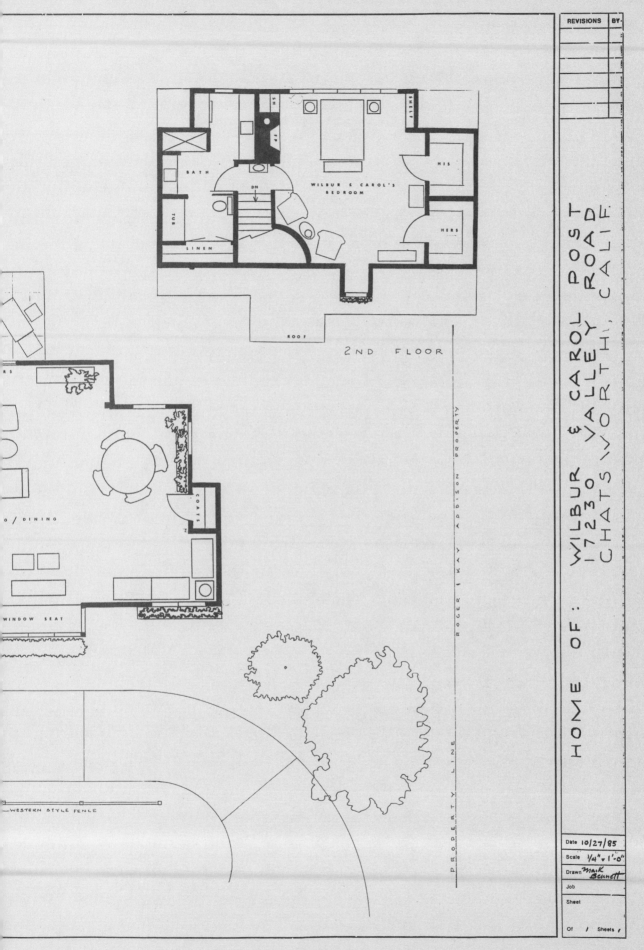

2ND FLOOR

BATH

TUB

LINEN

WILBUR & CAROL'S BEDROOM

HIS

HERS

ROOF

DN

ROGER & KAY ADDISON PROPERTY

PROPERTY LINE

/ DINING

COATS

WINDOW SEAT

WESTERN STYLE FENCE

REVISIONS   BY

HOME OF: WILBUR & CAROL POST
17230 VALLEY ROAD
CHATSWORTH, CALIF.

Date 10/27/85
Scale 1/4" = 1'-0"
Drawn Mark Bennett
Job
Sheet
Of / Sheets /

"MISTER ED"

27

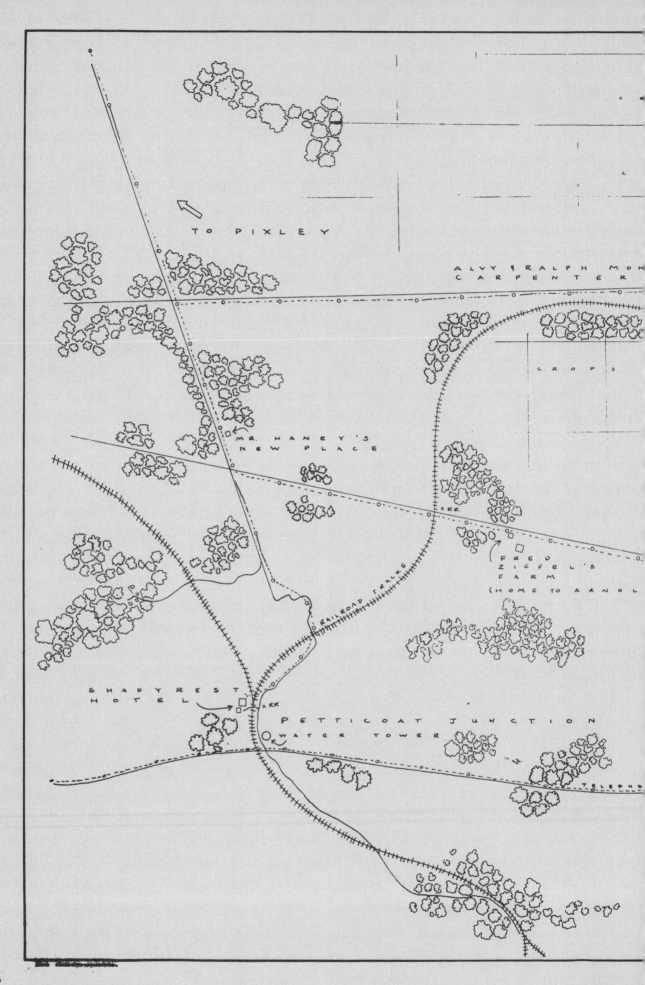

TO PIXLEY

ALVY & RALPH MON
CARPENTER

CROPS

MR. HANEY'S
NEW PLACE

X RR

FRED
ZIFFEL'S
FARM
(HOME TO ARNOL

RAILROAD TRACKS

SHADY REST
HOTEL
X RR

PETTICOAT JUNCTION
WATER TOWER

TELEPHO

28

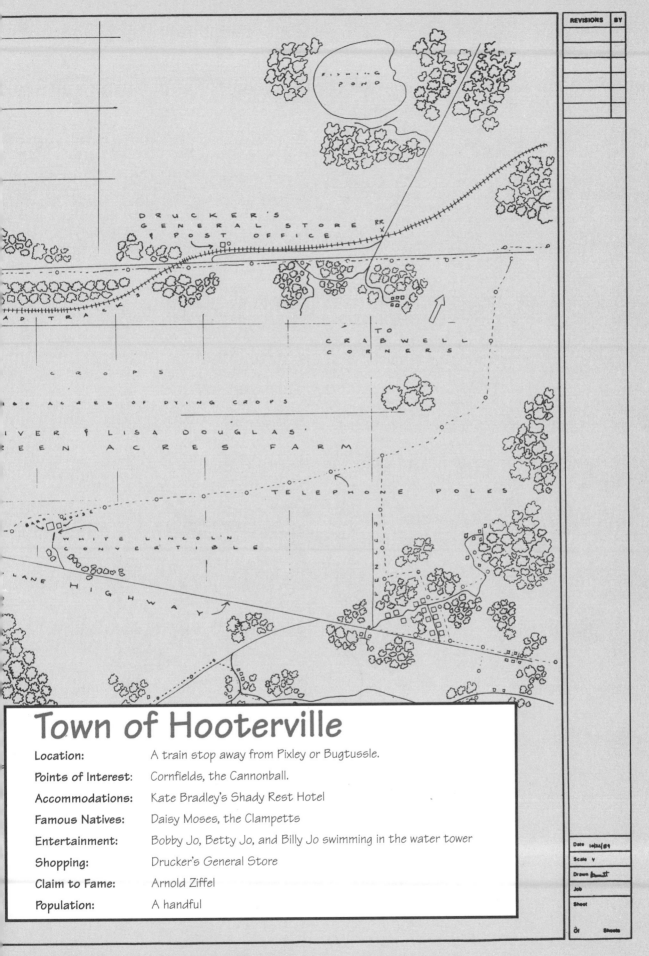

REVISIONS | BY

Date 10/22/89
Scale V
Drawn Bennett
Job
Sheet
of   Sheets

Town of Hooterville

Location:	A train stop away from Pixley or Bugtussle.
Points of Interest:	Cornfields, the Cannonball.
Accommodations:	Kate Bradley's Shady Rest Hotel
Famous Natives:	Daisy Moses, the Clampetts
Entertainment:	Bobby Jo, Betty Jo, and Billy Jo swimming in the water tower
Shopping:	Drucker's General Store
Claim to Fame:	Arnold Ziffel
Population:	A handful

"GREEN ACRES" & "PETTICOAT JUNCTION"

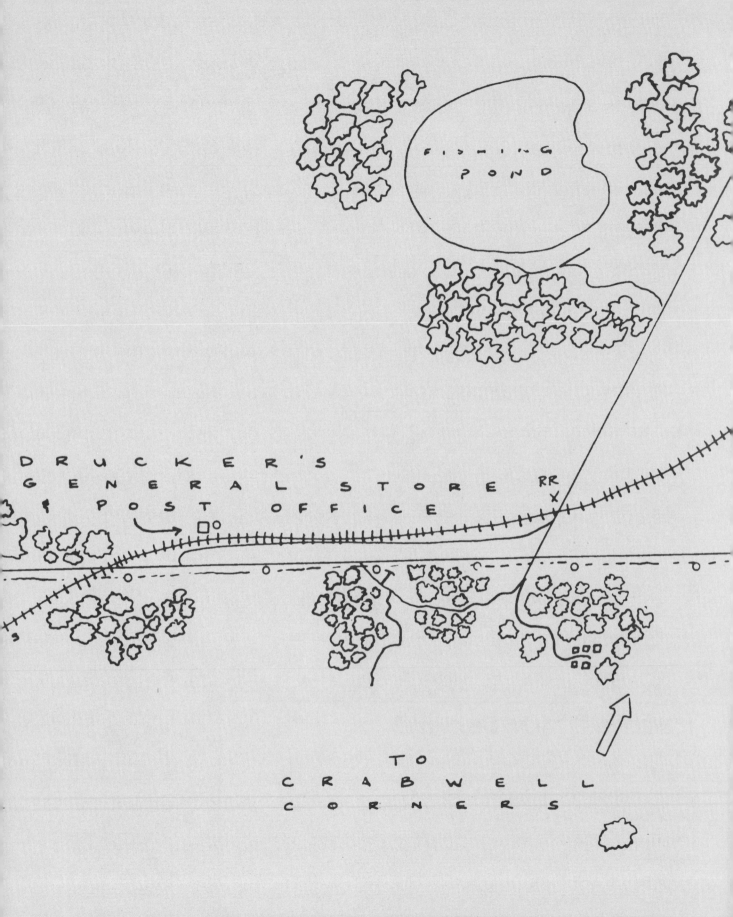

"GREEN ACRES"

Home of Oliver & Lisa Douglas

For a farmhouse, the Douglases of New York City did the best they could. This place is rough with a capital 'R.' A farm, bought from the local scam artist Mr. Haney, comes complete with a rusty tractor, a sagging barn, a hired hand named Ebb, many acres of withering crops and a clapboard farmhouse sans driveway.

It seems this house is always in a transition period of repair with an inept construction crew, headed up by the Monroe Brothers. There are holes in the kitchen floor, far too few electrical outlets, and a fireplace mantle held together with a little spit and lots of hope.

The living room is adorned with important artwork, designer furniture (such as a leopard-skin couch), cut-glass chandeliers and two burned-out floor sconces on either side of the fireplace.

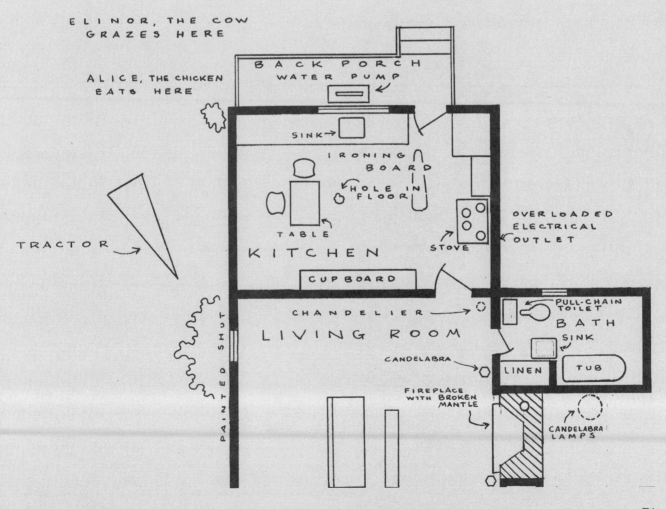

ELINOR, THE COW GRAZES HERE

ALICE, THE CHICKEN EATS HERE

BACK PORCH
WATER PUMP

SINK →

IRONING BOARD

HOLE IN FLOOR

TRACTOR →

TABLE

KITCHEN

STOVE

OVERLOADED ELECTRICAL OUTLET

CUPBOARD

PAINTED SHUT

CHANDELIER →

LIVING ROOM

CANDELABRA →

PULL-CHAIN TOILET

BATH

SINK →

LINEN

TUB

FIREPLACE WITH BROKEN MANTLE →

CANDELABRA LAMPS

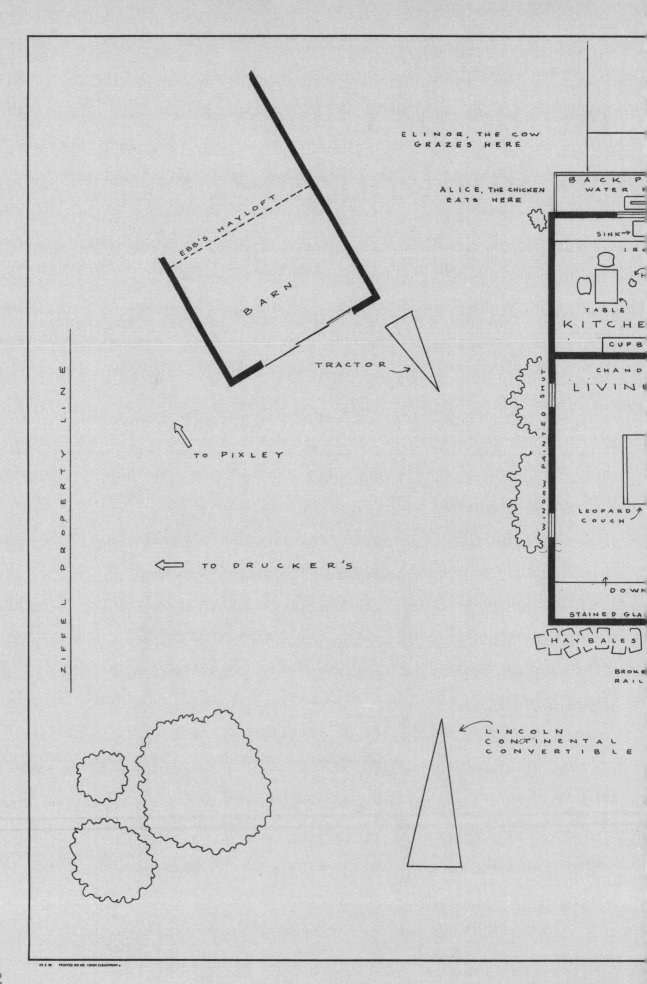

ELINOR, THE COW
GRAZES HERE

ALICE, THE CHICKEN
EATS HERE

BACK P

WATER

SINK →

I R

TABLE

KITCHE

CUPB

CHAND

LIVING

WINDOW PAINTED SHUT

LEOPARD
COUCH →

DOWN

STAINED GLA

HAY BALES

BROKE
RAIL

EBB'S HAYLOFT

BARN

TRACTOR

TO PIXLEY

TO DRUCKER'S

ZIFFEL PROPERTY LINE

LINCOLN
CONTINENTAL
CONVERTIBLE

24 X 36   PRINTED ON NO. 1000H CLEARPRINT ®

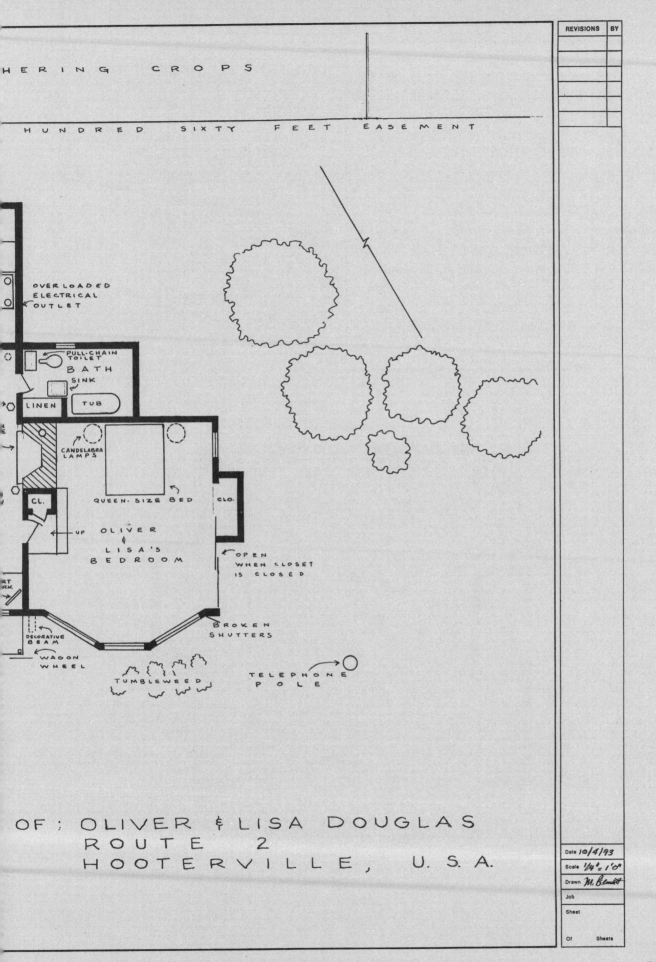

WHERING CROPS

HUNDRED SIXTY FEET EASEMENT

OVERLOADED
ELECTRICAL
OUTLET

PULL-CHAIN
TOILET
BATH
SINK
LINEN
TUB

CANDELABRA
LAMPS

CL.

QUEEN-SIZE BED

CLO.

UP OLIVER
&
LISA'S
BEDROOM

OPEN
WHEN CLOSET
IS CLOSED

DECORATIVE
BEAM

BROKEN
SHUTTERS

WAGON
WHEEL

TUMBLEWEED

TELEPHONE
POLE

OF: OLIVER & LISA DOUGLAS
ROUTE 2
HOOTERVILLE, U.S.A.

REVISIONS | BY

Date 10/4/93
Scale 1/4"= 1'0"
Drawn M. Blanitt
Job
Sheet
Of   Sheets

The bedroom has unfinished walls, a closet filled with expensive labels and no exterior wall, an elaborate headboard surrounded by more chandeliers hanging from crumbling ceilings. Farm animals have the run of the place, and the best form of communicating with the outside world is via the semi-convenient telephone atop the nearby power pole.

You have to hand it to Lisa and Oliver. What troopers. To trade the fast-paced, big-city life for a little fresh air, even if Lisa is allergic to hay bales, shows real intestinal fortitude. Anyone who would leave the comforts of a Park Avenue penthouse to reside in a 900-square-foot shanty deserves to drive a white-on-white Lincoln convertible.

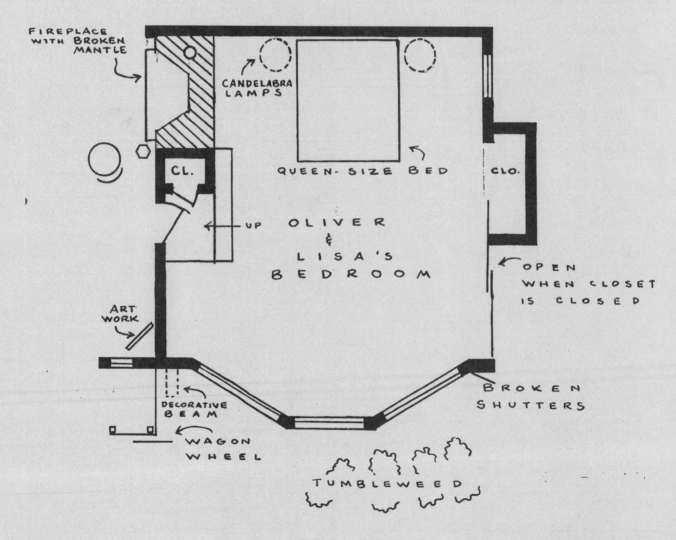

FIREPLACE WITH BROKEN MANTLE

CANDELABRA LAMPS

CL.

QUEEN-SIZE BED

CLO.

UP OLIVER & LISA'S BEDROOM

OPEN WHEN CLOSET IS CLOSED

ART WORK

DECORATIVE BEAM

WAGON WHEEL

BROKEN SHUTTERS

TUMBLEWEED

"GREEN ACRES"

"THE ANDY GRIFFITH SHOW"
Town of Mayberry

Entering the peaceful town of Mayberry, probably on Highway Six past the sign that says, "Welcome to Mayberry, the Friendly Town," the motorist might first stop at Wally's Gas Station for a fill-up and soda pop. Lush trees, clean air, Emma Brand's homey cabin overlooking Myer's Lake—you would think you've driven into an environment of Southern charm and endless summer days. It's all true.

Pass the county fairgrounds and the old Palmerston Drive-In Theatre, and a right on Elm Street will take you toward the town. At 411 Elm, you can wave at Barney's bachelor digs at Mrs. Mendelbright's Rooming House. A right on Maple will take you past Sheriff Andy Taylor's modest home and the sweet smells of Aunt Bee's culinary delights. Clara Edwards lives next door, Nurse Peggy (her house is later sold to Helen Crump) down the street, and two blocks further on, Mayberry Water & Power.

Heading south on Maple and hanging a quick right on Main Street takes you into the hub of Mayberry activity: Foley's Market, Floyd's Barber Shop, the courthouse, the Bluebird Diner. It is very quaint here, brick buildings with flower boxes and street benches and citizens playing checkers in front of the Mayberry Hotel. Weaver's Department Store offers the shopper the ultimate in dry goods, and the Snappy Lunch has daily specials with refreshments such as lemon phosphate.

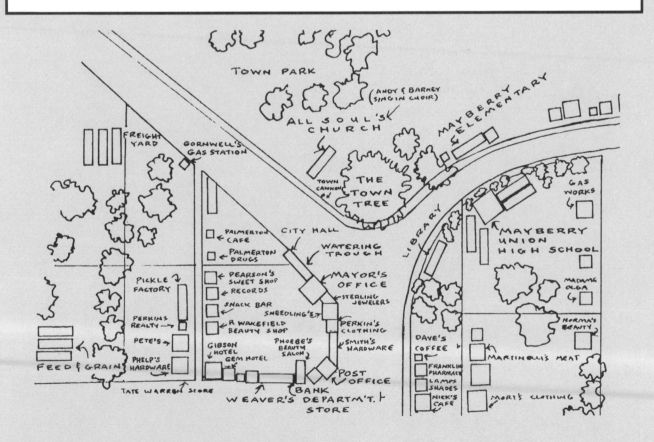

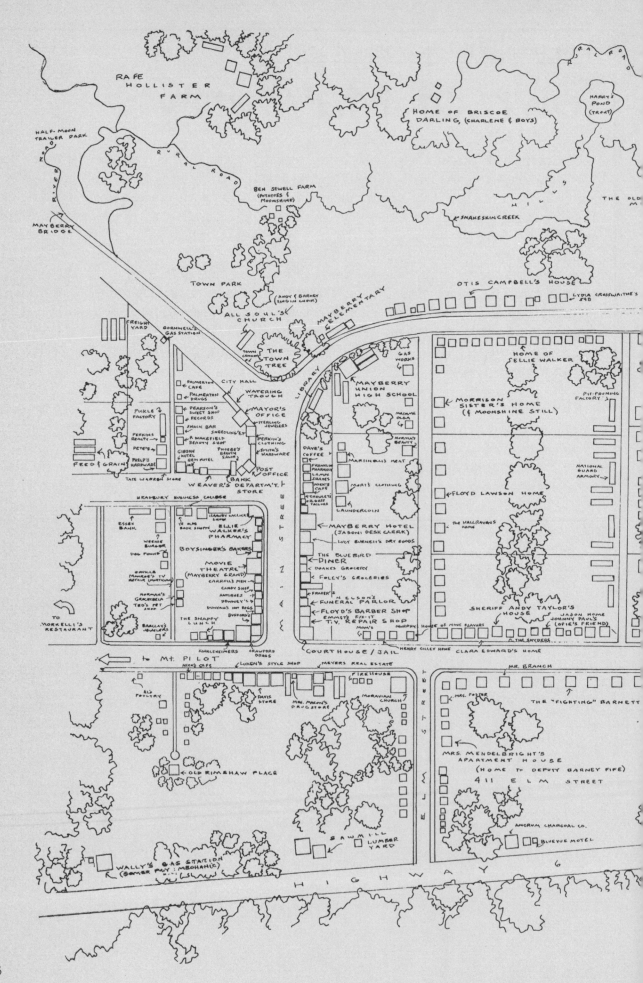

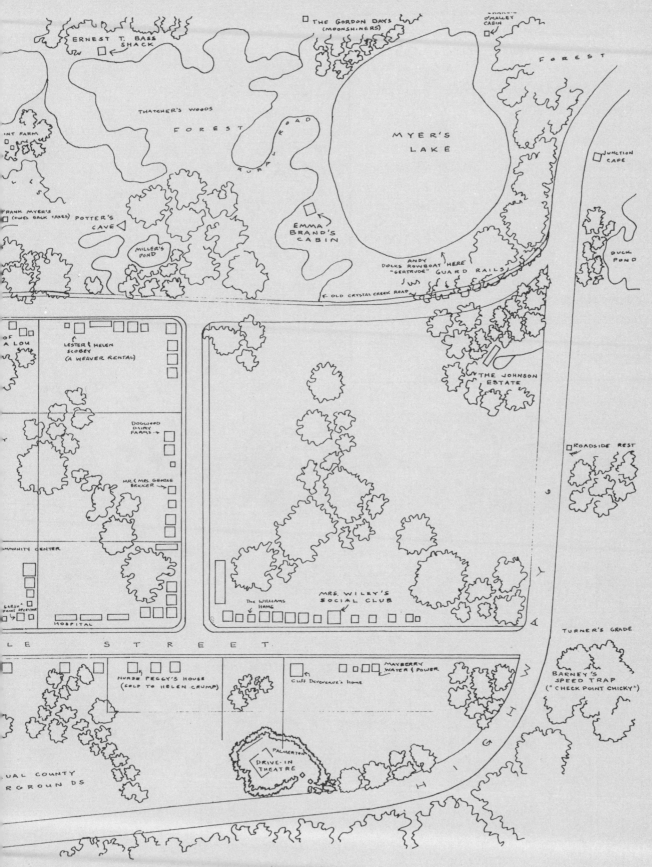

THE GORDON DAYS
(MOONSHINERS)

O'MALLEY CABIN

ERNEST T. BASS
SHACK

FOREST

THATCHER'S WOODS

FOREST

MYER'S
LAKE

BURP ROAD

JUNCTION
CAFE

NT FARM

FRANK MYER'S
(OWES BACK TAXES)   POTTER'S
CAVE

MILLER'S
POND

EMMA
BRAND'S
CABIN

ANDY
DOCKS ROWBOAT HERE
"GERTRUDE"   GUARD RAILS

DUCK
POND

F. OLD CRYSTAL CREEK ROAD

OF
A LOU

LESTER & HELEN
SCOBEY
(A WEAVER RENTAL)

THE JOHNSON
ESTATE

DOGWOOD
DAIRY
FARMS →

ROADSIDE REST

MR & MRS GEORGE
BRUKER →

MMUNITY CENTER

MRS. WILEY'S
SOCIAL CLUB

ARSH
PANE OFFICIAL

The WILLIAMS
HOME

HOSPITAL

TURNER'S GRADE

LE   S T R E E T

NURSE PEGGY'S HOUSE
(SOLD TO HELEN CRUMP)

CLIFF DEVEREAUX'S HOME

MAYBERRY
WATER & POWER

BARNEY'S
SPEED TRAP
("CHECK POINT CHICKY")

UAL COUNTY
RGROUNDS

PALMERTON
DRIVE-IN
THEATRE

H I G H W A Y

OWN of MAYBERRY,
NORTH CAROLINA, U.S.A.

You could live here. Everyone offers a friendly hello, a warm smile, a covered dish to welcome you to the community. A Greyhound bus stops every day on Main Street and traffic is almost nonexistent.

You'll see all the locals on Sunday at the All Soul's Church; Rafe Hollister will sing a hymn and the Morrison Sisters might invite you home for Sunday dinner and a fresh batch of their home brew.

There are favorite fishing holes, the old Johnson mine, Potter's cave and the Spooky Rimshaw House to explore. If you get really bored, you can talk to Sarah, the phone operator. And if it gets really stale, there's always Mt. Pilot.

TURNER'S GRADE

BARNEY'S SPEED TRAP ("CHECK POINT CHICKY

SPEED LIMIT 45

Z SHOP HOP MURPHY'S HOUSE OF NINE FLAVORS

SHERIFF ANDY TAYLOR'S HOUSE

JASON HOME JOHNNY PAUL'S (OPIE'S FRIEND)

THE SNYDERS

HENRY GILLEY HOME CLARA EDWARD'S HOME

IL

MR. BRANCH

MRS. FOSTER

THE "FIGHTING" BARNETTS

GROVE ST

MRS. MENDELBRIGHT'S APARTMENT HOUSE (HOME TO DEPUTY BARNEY FIFE) 411 ELM STREET

"THE ANDY GRIFFITH SHOW"

Home of Andy Taylor

At 322 Maple, in the town of Mayberry, is a comfortable two-story wood and shingle house near town, This is the residence of local sheriff Andy Taylor, his son Opie and Aunt Bee.

Large trees grace the front yard. A driveway runs to the right of the house and ends at a detached single-car garage at the rear of the property. A wide set of wooden porch steps leads to a veranda. There you will find a rocker, wicker porch furniture, hanging ferns, a nice summer breeze, the lull of crickets. A perfect place to take a nap.

Inside, the visitor enters an L-shaped living/dining area featuring a large stone fireplace with a deer head above the mantle on the rear wall. The upholstered couch and chairs are centrally located in the center of the room and have the homey addition of doilies on the backs and arms. A black telephone rests on an end table. There is a spinet piano against the wall, near the coat table. The dining area is paneled and has a table with four Windsor chairs and a china hutch.

The kitchen is small, with a crank telephone, a breakfast table and chairs, refrigerator, and a temperamental freezer on the service porch. The gas oven works lots of overtime.

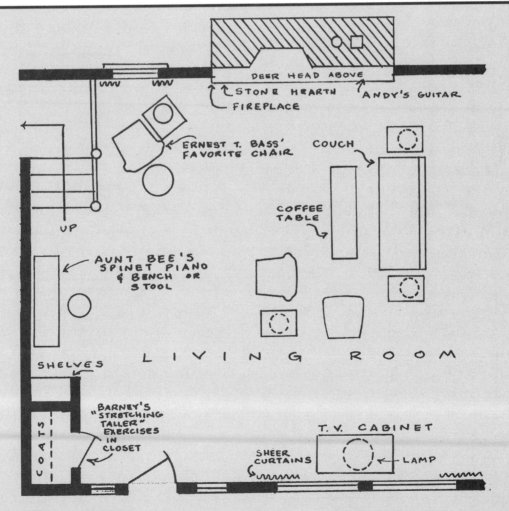

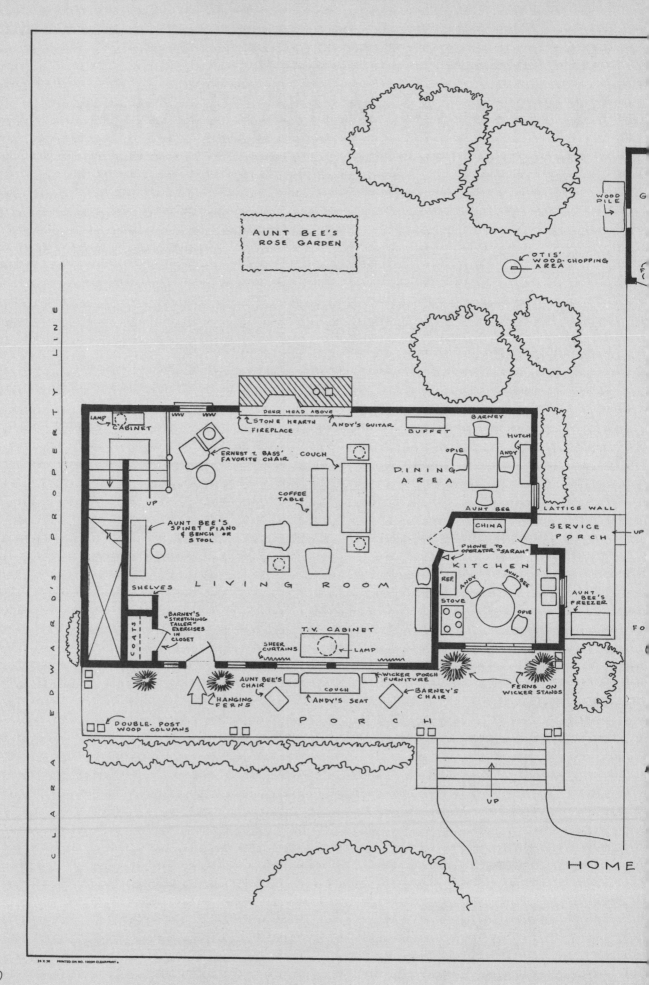

AUNT BEE'S
ROSE GARDEN

WOOD
PILE

OTIS'
WOOD-CHOPPING
AREA

LAMP
CABINET

DEER HEAD ABOVE
STONE HEARTH
FIREPLACE   ANDY'S GUITAR

BUFFET   BARNEY

HUTCH

OPIE   ANDY

ERNEST T. BASS'
FAVORITE CHAIR   COUCH

DINING
AREA

AUNT BEE

LATTICE WALL

UP

COFFEE
TABLE

CHINA

SERVICE
PORCH

PHONE TO
OPERATOR "SARAH"

AUNT BEE'S
SPINET PIANO
& BENCH OR
STOOL

KITCHEN

REF.   ANDY   AUNT BEE

STOVE

AUNT
BEE'S
FREEZER

SHELVES   L I V I N G   R O O M

OPIE

BARNEY'S
"STRETCHING
TALLER"
EXERCISES
IN
CLOSET

COATS

T.V. CABINET

SHEER
CURTAINS   LAMP

DOUBLE-POST
WOOD COLUMNS

AUNT BEE'S
CHAIR

HANGING
FERNS

COUCH

ANDY'S SEAT

WICKER PORCH
FURNITURE

BARNEY'S
CHAIR

FERNS ON
WICKER STANDS

P O R C H

UP

HOME

40

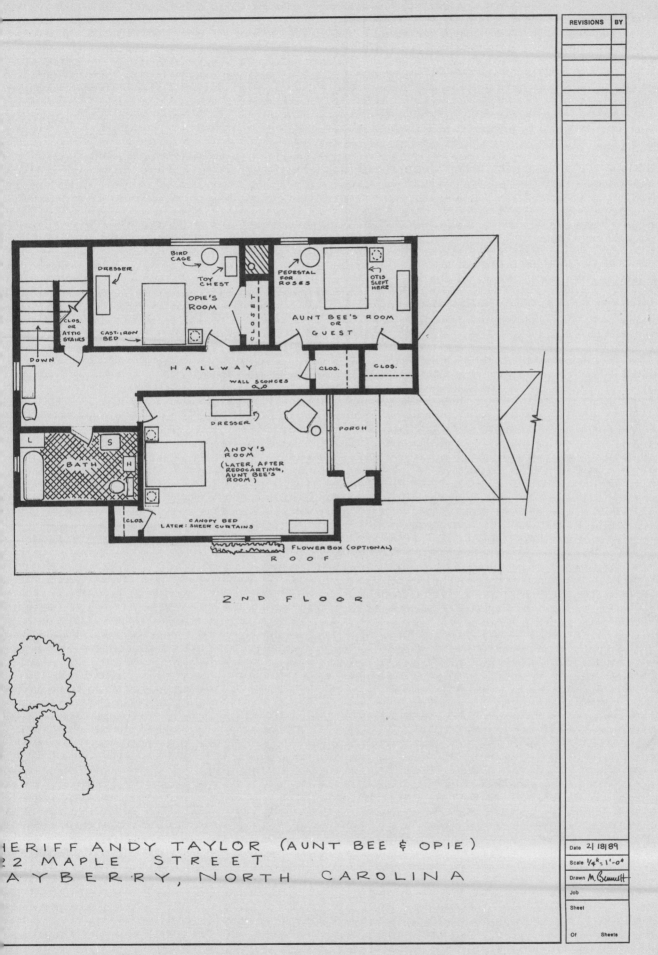

DRESSER

BIRD
CAGE

TOY
CHEST

PEDESTAL
FOR
ROSES

OTIS
SLEPT
HERE

CLOS.
OR
ATTIC
STAIRS

OPIE'S
ROOM

AUNT BEE'S ROOM
OR
GUEST

CAST-IRON
BED

DOWN

HALLWAY

CLOS.

CLOS.

WALL SCONCES

DRESSER

PORCH

L

S

BATH

H

ANDY'S
ROOM

(LATER, AFTER
REDECORATING,
AUNT BEE'S
ROOM)

CLOS

CANOPY BED
LATER: SHEER CURTAINS

FLOWERBOX (OPTIONAL)

ROOF

2ND FLOOR

SHERIFF ANDY TAYLOR (AUNT BEE & OPIE)
22 MAPLE STREET
MAYBERRY, NORTH CAROLINA

Date 2|18|89
Scale 1/4" = 1'-0"
Drawn M. Bennett
Job
Sheet
Of   Sheets

Upstairs, there are three bedrooms large enough to have guests stay over. Let's see: there was the time Cousin Gloria came to visit, and the week that Uncle Ollie and Aunt Nora brought the boys for a spell, and the time Otis had to serve out of his jail time, and when Gomer lost his room behind Wally's Service Station and when Ernest T. Bass got his makeover.

There are nice dinners served here almost every night. Aunt Bee makes home-made pickles and jams and her pies are legendary. It's comfortable, peaceful, quiet. You won't order cocktails here. Mayberry is a dry county. There may be a bar with a floor show over in Yancey, or beer by the glass in Mt. Pilot, but you won't find as hospitable a home to spend an evening in.

AUNT BEE'S ROSE GARDEN

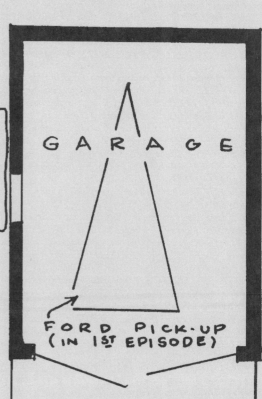

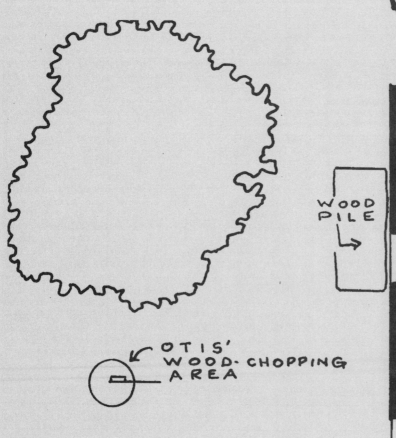

← OTIS' WOOD-CHOPPING AREA

WOOD PILE →

G A R A G E

FORD PICK-UP (IN 1ST EPISODE)

"THE ANDY GRIFFITH SHOW"

"THE BIG VALLEY"

Home of Victoria Barkley

If you are ever in Stockton, a showplace home to see would be the Barkley Ranch. A stately manor with stables, this spread even has a working fountain out front.

Big columns flank the entrance, supporting a two-story portico. French doors on the first and second floor. A balcony above the main entrance. There is no doubt Victoria could throw a serious party here.

Inside a grand foyer, one step down, there is a magnificent sweeping staircase. To the right, and through double doors, a large library for lawyer son Jerrod offers up chairs of real leather and quill pens galore. A parlor decorated in turn-of-the-century furniture is off to the left: a large, high-ceilinged room with generous use of potted plants in the corners.

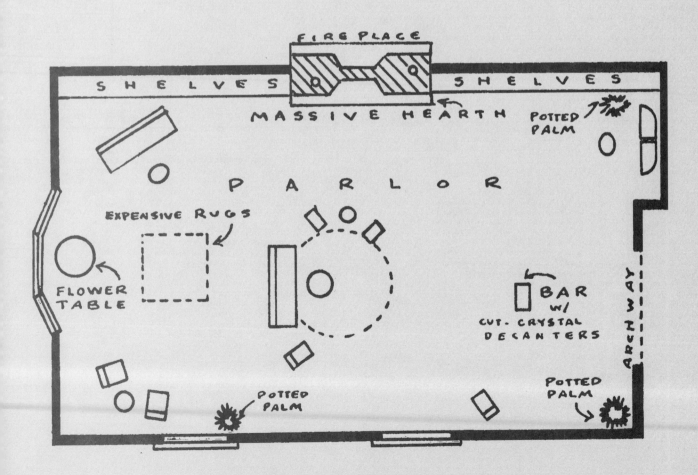

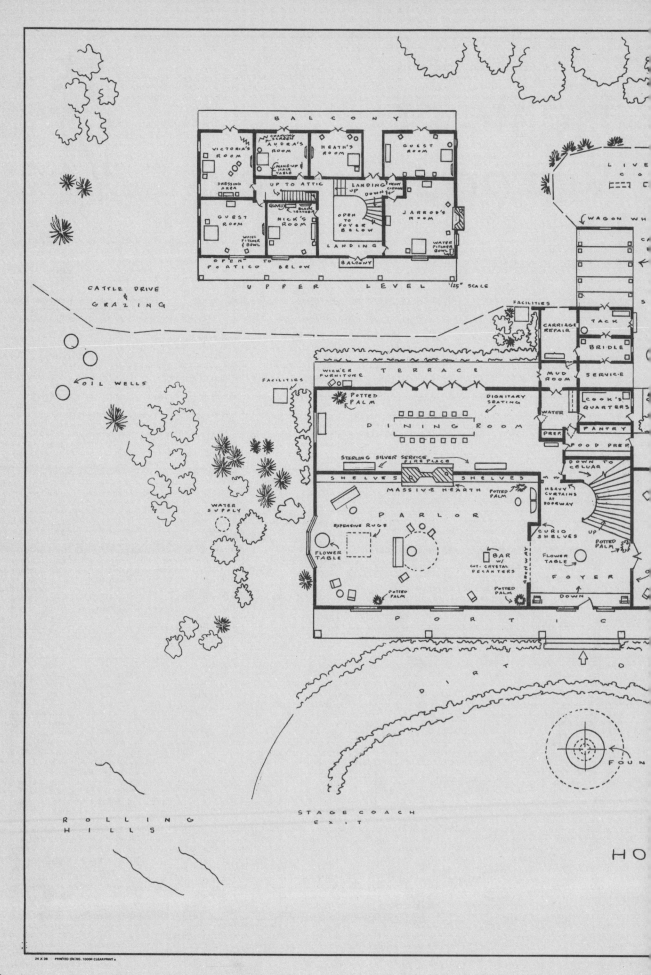

BALCONY

VICTORIA'S ROOM

DRESSING AREA

AUDRA'S ROOM

CHANGING SCREEN

MAKE-UP & HAIR TABLE

HEATH'S ROOM

GUEST ROOM

UP TO ATTIC

LANDING UP

LANDING DOWN

HEAVY CURTAINS

GUEST ROOM

NICK'S ROOM

WATER PITCHER & BOWL

GLOVES

BLACK LEATHER

OPEN TO FOYER BELOW

JARROD'S ROOM

WATER PITCHER & BOWL

OPEN TO PORTICO BELOW

LANDING

BALCONY

UPPER LEVEL   1/25" SCALE

CATTLE DRIVE & GRAZING

OIL WELLS

WATER SUPPLY

LIVE CO

WAGON WH

FACILITIES

CARRIAGE REPAIR

TACK

BRIDLE

MUD ROOM

SERVICE

FACILITIES

WICKER FURNITURE   TERRACE

POTTED PALM

DIGNITARY SEATING

WATER

COOK'S QUARTERS

DINING ROOM

PREP

PANTRY

FOOD PREP

STERLING SILVER SERVICE

FIREPLACE

DOWN TO CELLAR

SHELVES

SHELVES

MASSIVE HEARTH

POTTED PALM

HEAVY CURTAINS AT DOORWAY

PARLOR

EXTENSIVE RUGS

CURIO SHELVES

UP

FLOWER TABLE

BAR w/ CUT CRYSTAL DECANTERS

FLOWER TABLE

POTTED PALM

FOYER

POTTED PALM

POTTED PALM

DOWN

PORTIC

DIRT D

FOUN

STAGE COACH EXIT

ROLLING HILLS

HO

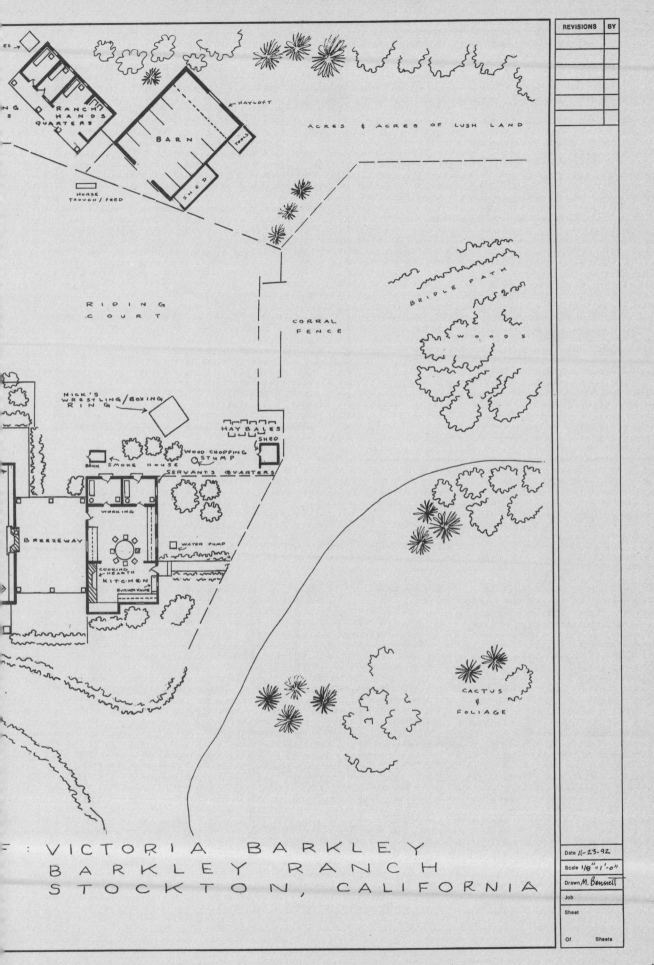

RANCH HANDS QUARTERS

← HAYLOFT

BARN

SHED

TOOLS

HORSE TROUGH / FEED

ACRES & ACRES OF LUSH LAND

RIDING COURT

CORRAL FENCE

BRIDLE PATH

WOODS

NICK'S WRESTLING/BOXING RING →

HAY BALES

SHED

WOOD CHOPPING STUMP

BRICK SMOKE HOUSE

SERVANTS QUARTERS

WORKING

BREEZEWAY

COOKING HEARTH

KITCHEN

BUTCHER KNIFE

WATER PUMP

CACTUS & FOLIAGE

F: VICTORIA BARKLEY
BARKLEY RANCH
STOCKTON, CALIFORNIA

REVISIONS | BY

Date 11-23-92
Scale 1/8" = 1'-0"
Drawn M. Bennett
Job
Sheet
Of   Sheets

"THE BIG VALLEY"

A formal dining room with seating for state dignitaries and V.I.P.s is off the working pantry. A separate smokehouse and prep kitchen are located conveniently off the main house.

Upstairs, there are master suites for Victoria, Nick, Audra, Heath, Jerrod—some with fireplaces, and all with armoires for smart Western outfits. Heavy, swag curtains drape most hallway entrances. The third-floor attic stores summer furniture and back-up cast-iron bed frames.

There are plenty of chores to do here. If you are not a servant you can enjoy many activities. There are horse stables, a livery, a riding circle, a branding pit, a livestock corral and Nick's wrestling ring.

What a joy to be a Barkley.

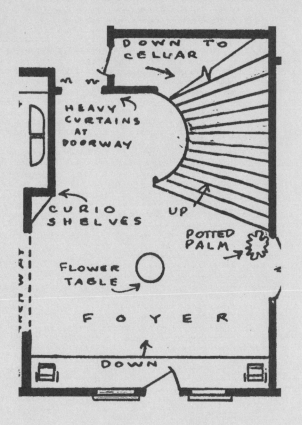

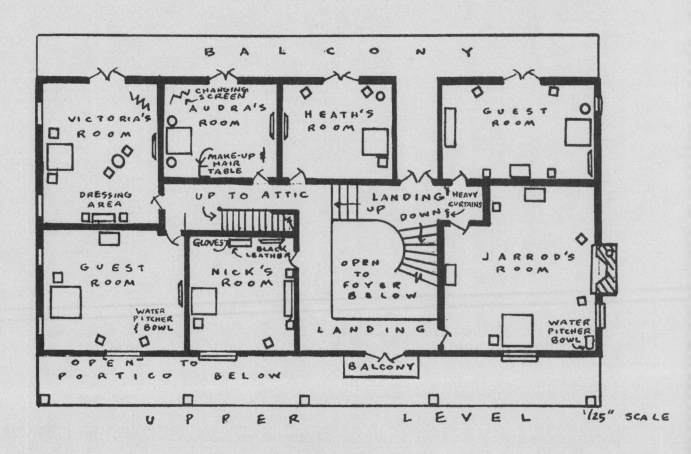

"THE BIG VALLEY"

"THE WILD, WILD WEST"

Train Coach Home of Jim West

The curtains are plush, festooned with many tassels. The couches are upholstered in sumptuous crush velvet. There is a bar, with a brass foot rail, and enough hidden gadgets to capture even the most notorious villain. Welcome to the mobile home of secret agent Jim West and his sidekick and man of a thousand disguises, Artemus Gordon. Be careful what you touch here. One false swoop over a desk-drawer knob and you might find an arsenal peeking out from every gold-plated Winchester statue.

A dining table converts into a planning table for a map territory strategy session. A small closet to the left of the bar is actually an arsenal with guns displayed behind moving partitions. There is even a cozy hutch above the door that houses Henry and Henrietta, Jim's two homing pigeons.

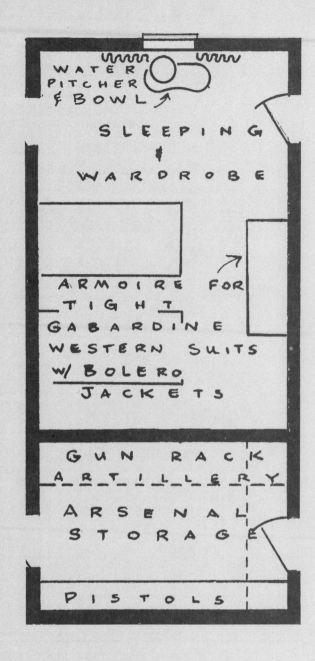

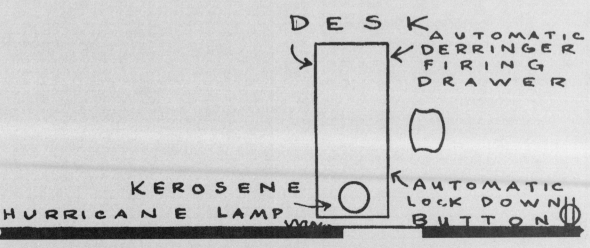

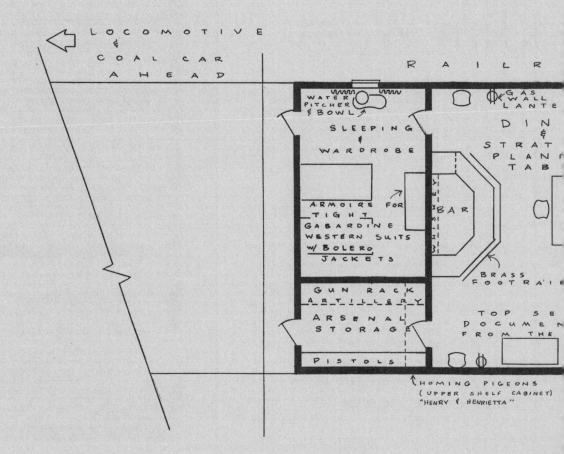

TO DODGE CITY

LOCOMOTIVE & COAL CAR AHEAD

RAILR

WATER PITCHER & BOWL

SLEEPING & WARDROBE

GAS WALL LANTE

DIN &
STRAT
PLAN
TAB

ARMOIRE FOR TIGHT GABARDINE WESTERN SUITS W/ BOLERO JACKETS

BAR

BRASS FOOTRAI

GUN RACK ARTILLERY

ARSENAL STORAGE

TOP SE
DOCUMEN
FROM THE

PISTOLS

HOMING PIGEONS
(UPPER SHELF CABINET)
"HENRY & HENRIETTA"

HOME OF

Sleeping quarters lie through a doorway to the right of the bar.

For a late-1800s boudoir, this converted boxcar is a rolling palace with a masculine touch. Lasso your horse up to the rear railing and step inside to a world of the politically powerful and morally weak. There will be nice fire going, and a telegram from the President on the settee. Pour yourself a brandy and slip into a smoking jacket. You finger a fully-loaded pearl-handle Derringer in your pocket and eye the surroundings. Crank up the Victrola. Feel good about bringing a date here.

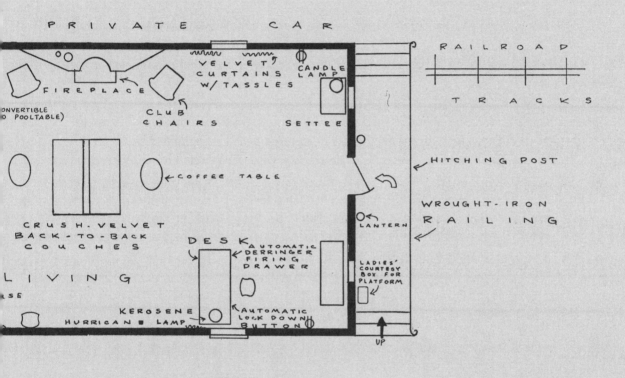

PRIVATE CAR

VELVET
CURTAINS
w/TASSLES

CANDLE
LAMP

FIREPLACE

CLUB
CHAIRS

SETTEE

ONVERTIBLE
O POOLTABLE)

COFFEE TABLE

CRUSH. VELVET
BACK-TO-BACK
COUCHES

DESK

AUTOMATIC
DERRINGER
FIRING
DRAWER

LIVING

SE

KEROSENE
HURRICANE LAMP

AUTOMATIC
LOCK DOWN
BUTTON

RAILROAD

TRACKS

HITCHING POST

WROUGHT-IRON
RAILING

LANTERN

LADIES'
COURTESY
BOX FOR
PLATFORM

UP

TO THE EVIL
DR. LOVELESS

AMES WEST/ARTEMUS GORDON
. S. A.

Ricardo Apartment— New York City

This converted brownstone at 623 East 68 Street in Manhattan is the home of Fred and Ethel Mertz, Mrs. Trumble, Grace Foster, and, of course, Lucy and Ricky Ricardo.

Before Little Ricky was born, Apartment 4A was perfect for the Ricardos. But when Mrs. Benson's daughter got married, Lucy and Ethel talked her into switching apartments. With the move, the Ricardos gained an extra bedroom and a large window in the living room. And a new apartment number, 3D.

The apartment is nicely furnished, updated every year or so with new furniture. An eat-in kitchen can be closed off from the living room by a set of louvered shutters mounted on the pass-through. There is a large bedroom with twin beds, a dressing area and bath, and a nursery for the baby.

No doubt this place has a history. There have been cocktail parties, business dinners, anniversaries, card games, home movies—why, basketball has been played in the living room. Even Superman dropped by for Little Ricky's fifth birthday party. And of course the Ladies' Wednesday Afternoon Fine Arts League meets here, too. On Thursdays.

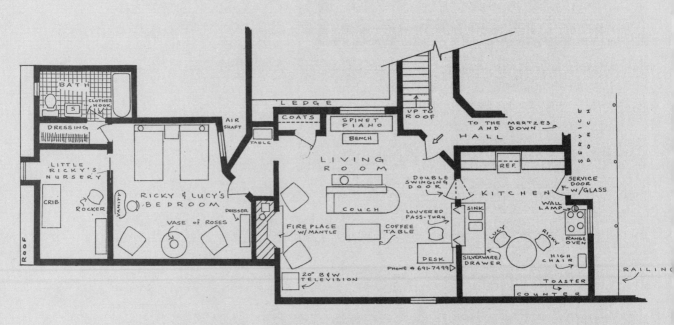

HOME OF: RICKY & LUCY RICARDO
623 EAST 68TH STREET
APT. 3D
NEW YORK, NEW YORK

"I LOVE LUCY"

The Ricardo Connecticut House

The picturesque two-acre property that the Ricardos have bought from Mr. and Mrs. Spalding is located in Westport, Connecticut. The main house is two-storied, with exposed beams, a sweeping staircase and hardwood floors. There is also a guest house, a chicken coop and a split-rail fence. A flagstone patio with privacy fence is off the kitchen, and, during their first year, the Ricardos and the Mertzes build a barbecue of brick.

A den with fireplace is off the main entrance, and it features a television in console cabinetry and a doorway out to a porch facing the street.

The house is decorated in early American furniture. There are hook rugs, Windsor chairs and dining table with Lazy Susan, a china hutch. Back-to-back couches, easy chairs, coffee tables, end tables—everything is impeccable. Thanks to Betty Ramsey, the new neighbor, and her friendship

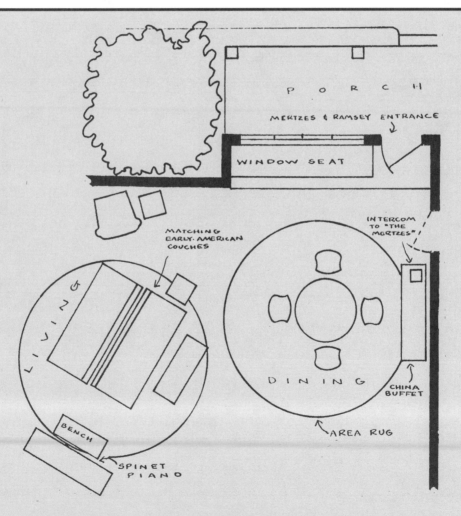

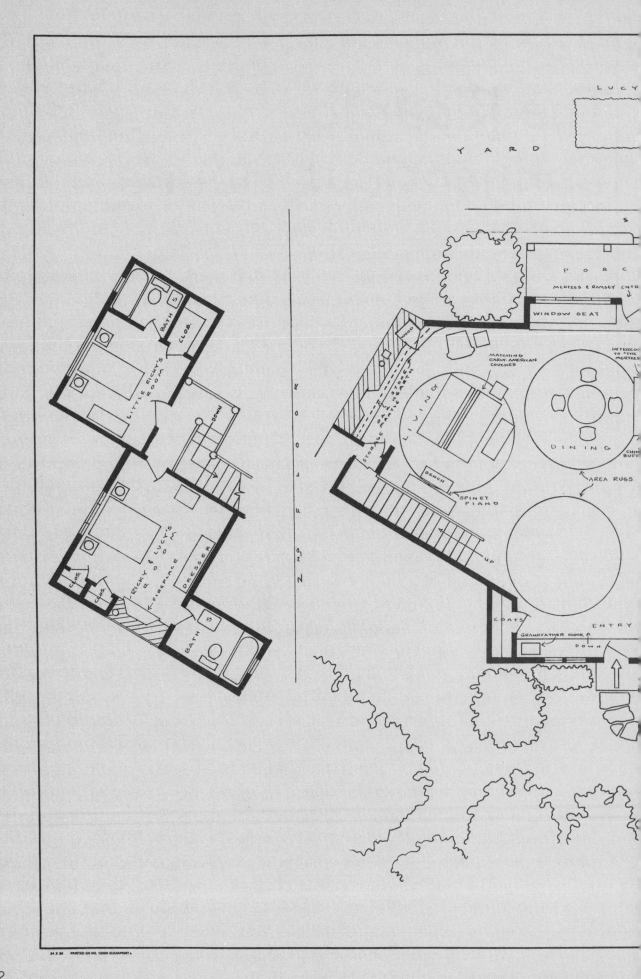

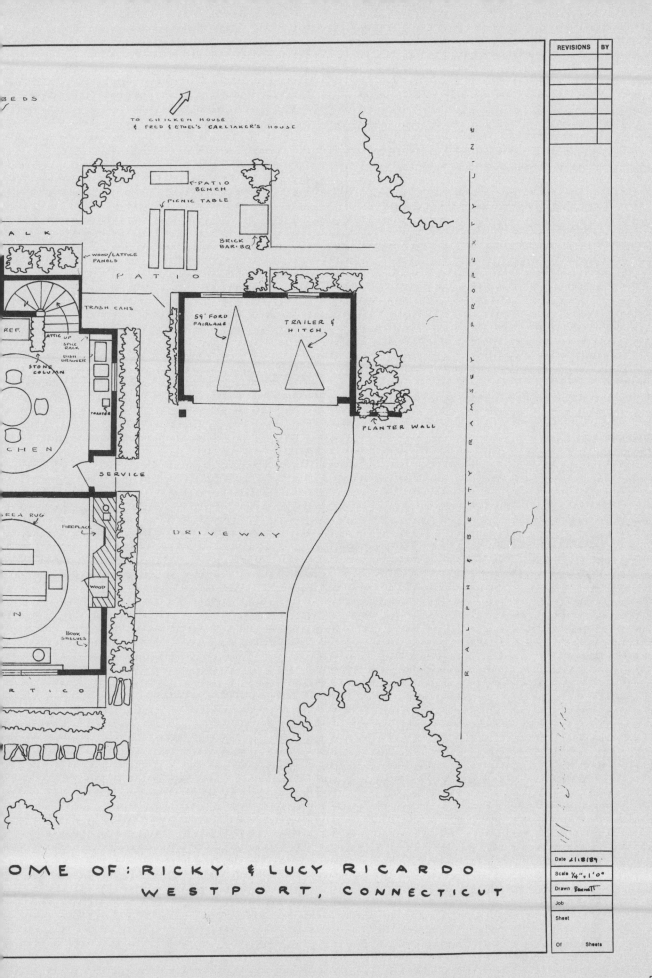

BEDS

TO CHICKEN HOUSE
& FRED & ETHEL'S CARETAKER'S HOUSE

PATIO
BENCH

PICNIC TABLE

BRICK
BAR-B-Q

WALK

WOOD/LATTICE
PANELS

PATIO

TRASH CANS

59' FORD
FAIRLANE

TRAILER &
HITCH

REF.

ATTIC UP
SPICE
RACK
DISH
DRAINER

STONE
COLUMN

TOASTER

PLANTER WALL

CHEN

SERVICE

AREA RUG

FIREPLACE

DRIVEWAY

WOOD

BOOK
SHELVES

N

RALPH & BETTY RAMSEY PROPERTY

RTICO

OME OF: RICKY & LUCY RICARDO
WESTPORT, CONNECTICUT

REVISIONS | BY

Date 1/18/89
Scale 1/4" = 1'0"
Drawn Bennett
Job
Sheet
Of   Sheets

"I LOVE LUCY"

with Mr. Perry, the furniture man, the Ricardo house becomes a candidate for a *House & Garden* magazine layout. Eggshell-colored pillow cushions complement the subtle plaid in the upholstered furniture. All that's missing is a rooster-based lamp. Later, Fred and Ethel consult Betty on redecorating the guest house.

Upstairs, there are bedrooms for Ricky and Lucy and one for Little Ricky. A spare bedroom is mentioned, but only the Mertzes get to stay in it the very first week they move to Westport. And thanks to Fred, the house, the guest house, and the chicken coop are all rigged with an intercom system.

With a 100-year-old fireplace with a woodbox and built-in bay window seating in the dining area, this country manse is a treasure. Rap on the door knocker. This house is warm and inviting.

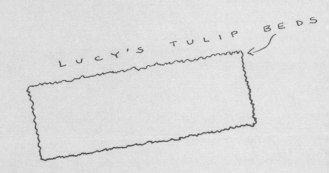

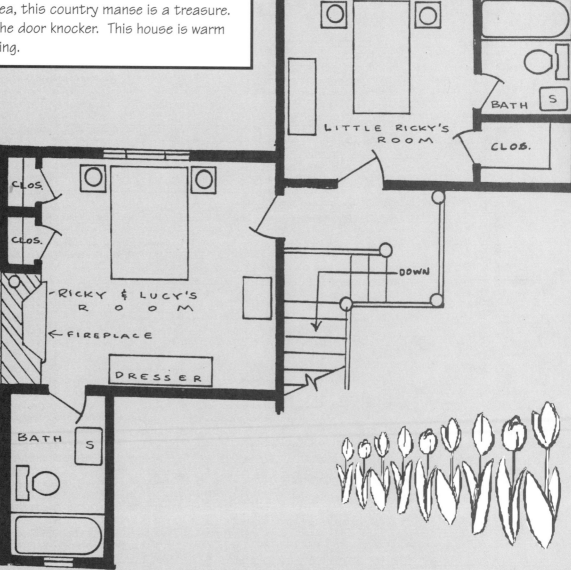

"I LOVE LUCY"

The Ricardo Beverly Palms Hotel Suite

In close proximity to MGM Studios, Suite 315 of the Beverly Palms Hotel becomes home to the Ricardos and Mrs. MacGuilicuddy for almost a year. The suite has a sweeping view of Hollywood, two bedrooms, even a kitchenette closed off by bi-fold partitions. The living room has striped horizontal wallpaper over support columns. With a built-in planter featuring starburst latticework, a Greta Grossman telephone table with a matching molded woven plywood chair, it's a wonder the Ricardos have time to wreak such havoc on Hollywood. Who'd ever want to leave this place?

If the sumptuous interiors of Suite 315 and, to an extent, the Mertzes' Suite 317 aren't enough, there is a pool outside with stars and starlets waiting to be discovered; Bobby, the bell-hop, at your beck and call; and a garage equipped with a brand-new 1956 Pontiac convertible and a courtesy air- and water-station.

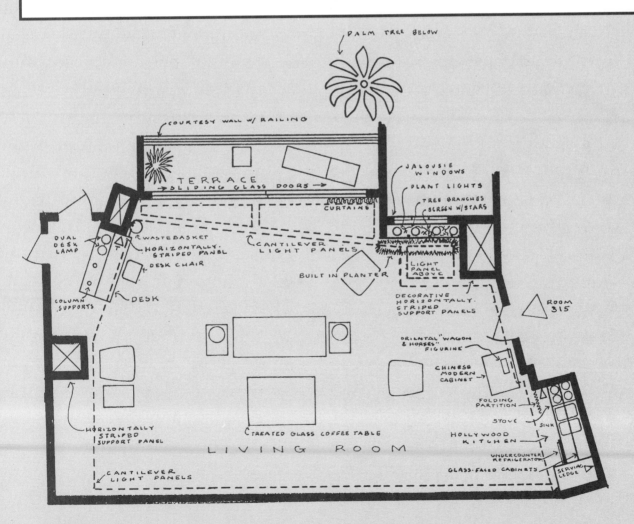

Laundry service, room service, maid service, the Ricardo suite seems to have it all. Even a lone palm tree by the terrace will break your fall if you decide to climb down from a fourth-floor balcony.

Hang out here and you might catch a glimpse of William Holden, John Wayne, Hedda Hopper or Harpo Marx. Check out Alan Ladd performing in the hotel ballroom. But don't look for Cornel Wilde. He checked out.

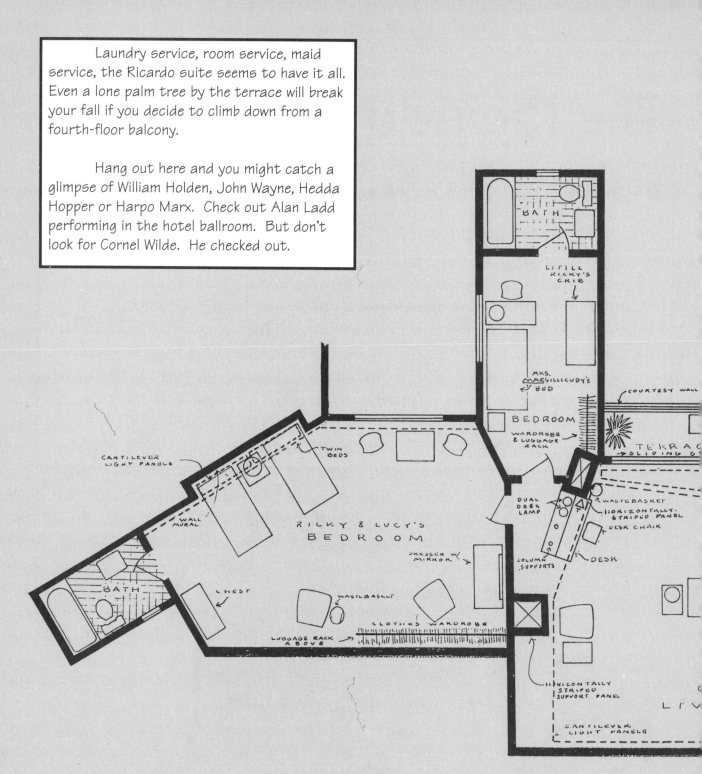

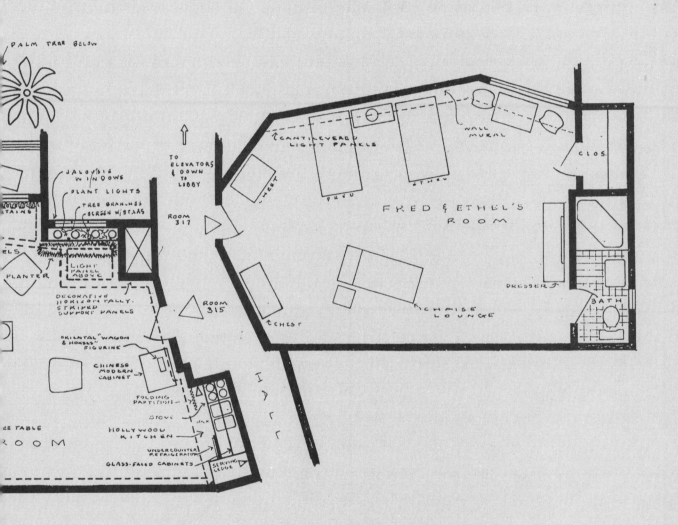

PALM TREE BELOW

JALOUSIE WINDOWS

PLANT LIGHTS

TREE BRANCHES
SCREEN W/STARS

TAINS

ELS

PLANTER

LIGHT PANEL ABOVE

DECORATIVE HORIZONTALLY STRIPED SUPPORT PANELS

ORIENTAL "WAGON & HORSES" FIGURINE

CHINESE MODERN CABINET

FOLDING PARTITION

STOVE

HOLLYWOOD KITCHEN

UNDERCOUNTER REFRIGERATOR

GLASS-FACED CABINETS

SERVING LEDGE

EE TABLE

ROOM

TO ELEVATORS & DOWN TO LOBBY

ROOM 317

ROOM 315

HALL

CANTILEVERED LIGHT PANELS

WALL MURAL

CLOS.

FRED

ETHEL

FRED & ETHEL'S ROOM

CHEST

CHEST

CHAISE LOUNGE

DRESSER

BATH

RICKY & LUCY RICARDO
℅ THE BEVERLY PALMS HOTEL
SUITE 315
HOLLYWOOD, CALIFORNIA

"FAMILY AFFAIR"

Home of William "Bill" Davis

Can't wait to get invited to a party here. Talk about opulence. This is the ultimate in snooty New York high-rise living. Double-door entry. One apartment per floor. Every kid should have the opportunity to be served breakfast on a tray by a distinguished butler on a terrace overlooking Central Park.

The home of Bill Davis, one of the most successful building contractors in Manhattan (and the world, for that matter), is breathtaking. Panels of inlaid-mahogany walls, two fireplaces (living room and den) and enough bedrooms to house two nieces and a nephew fresh from Terre Haute, Indiana, the Davis residence spells success. Built-in bookshelves, wall-to-wall carpeting, a butler's quarters and impressive reception area, this Manhattan apartment, high above Fifth Avenue, boasts panoramic views and enough closet space to house all those Abercrombie & Fitch hunting clothes. If you want to leave the city, a new Pontiac Bonneville station wagon is parked in the subterranean garage.

So what if your uncle is gone for three months building that swank hotel in Peru? You could probably hole up here for a year.

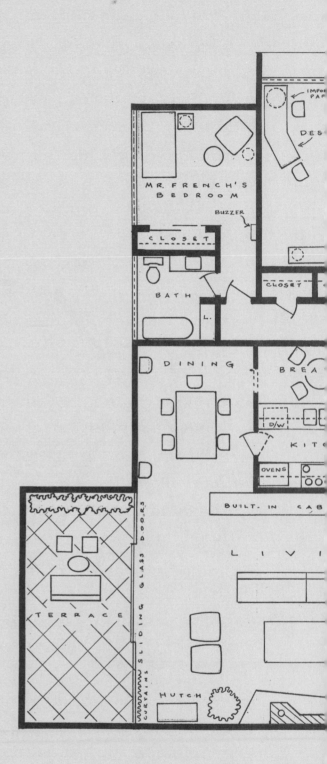

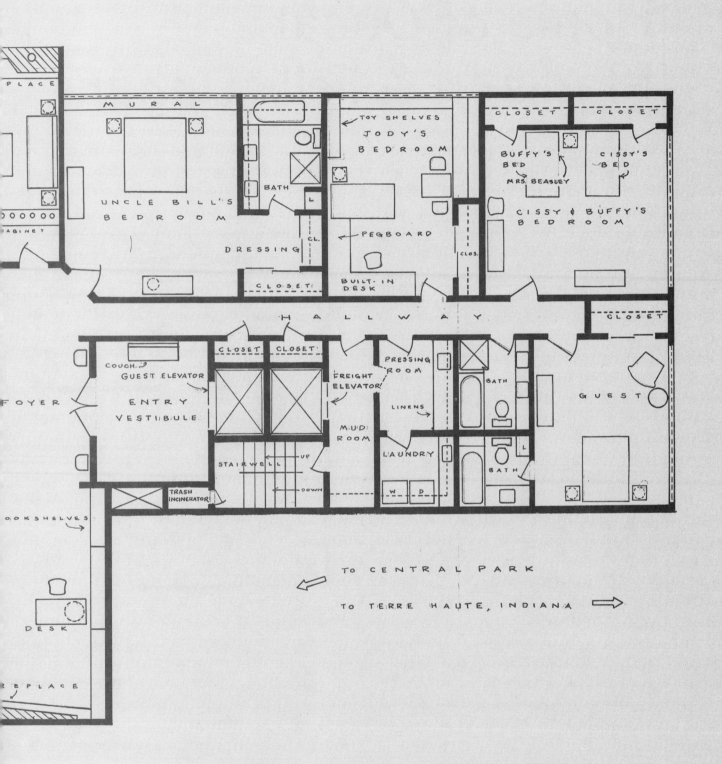

HOME OF: WILLIAM "BILL" DAVIS
NEW YORK, NEW YORK

"THE ODD COUPLE"

Home of Oscar Madison & Felix Ungar

This pre-war brick building with a doorman and entrance canopy is on the tony part of Park Avenue in Manhattan. Upstairs, you will find the Oscar Madison apartment: a two-bedroom flat with a step-down living-room, an eat-in kitchen and built-in bookshelves. Being the home of a sportswriter, there is a large desk with typewriter, a wastebasket and an ashtray brimming with cigar butts.

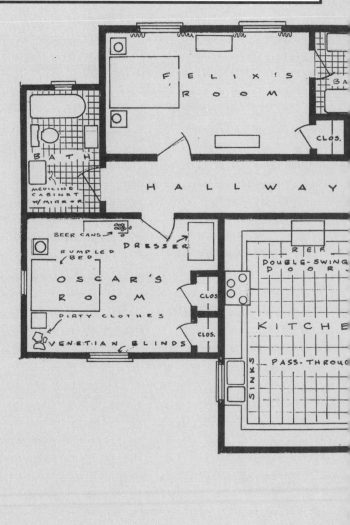

POKER PLAYED HERE

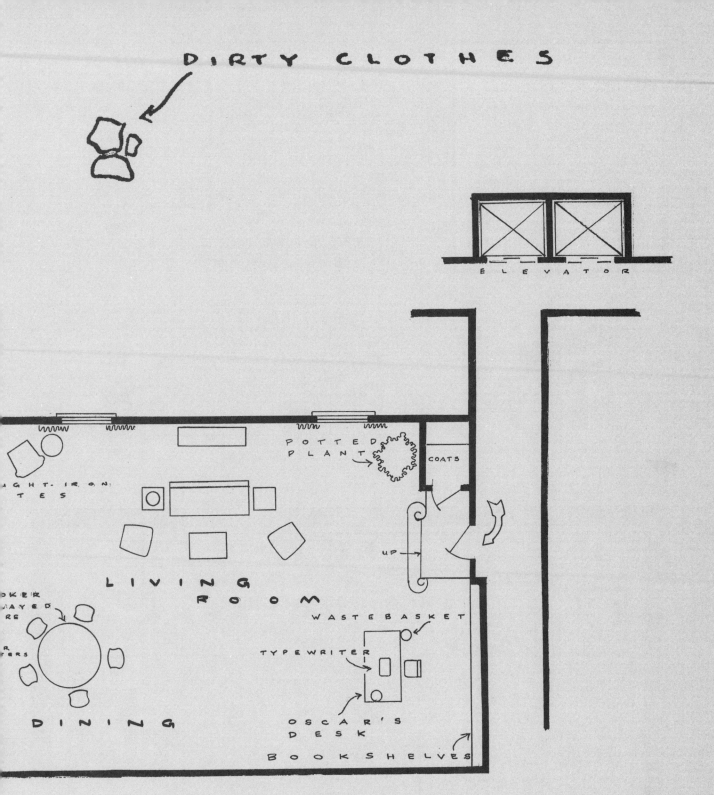

DIRTY CLOTHES

ELEVATOR

POTTED PLANT

COATS

WROUGHT-IRON GATES

UP

LIVING ROOM

WASTEBASKET

POKER PLAYED HERE

TYPEWRITER

CHAIRS

OSCAR'S DESK

DINING

BOOKSHELVES

HOME OF: OSCAR MADISON &
FELIX UNGAR
1049 PARK AVENUE
NEW YORK, NEW YORK

Then Felix moves in when his wife kicks him out. Suddenly, the carpet is vacuumed, the kitchen counters are spotless and the rooms are air-scented fresh. Now if you want to find a half-full can of beer, you've got to go to Oscar's room. Down the hall. Last door on the left.

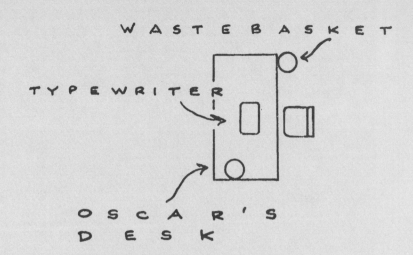

WASTEBASKET

TYPEWRITER

OSCAR'S DESK

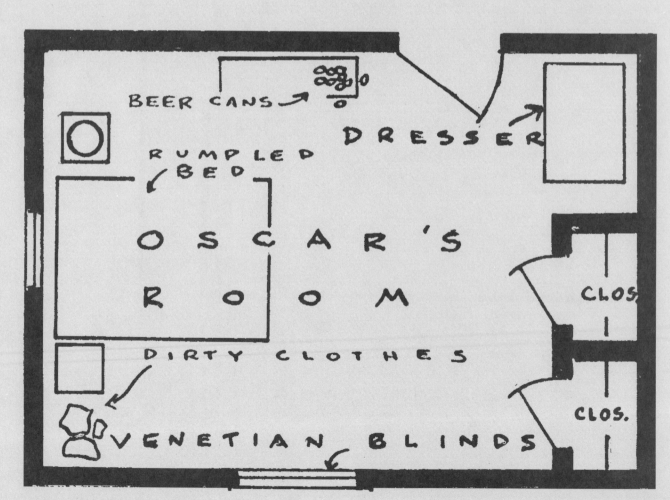

BEER CANS

DRESSER

RUMPLED BED

OSCAR'S ROOM

DIRTY CLOTHES

CLOS.

CLOS.

VENETIAN BLINDS

"THE ODD COUPLE"

The Clampett Mansion

The Clampett Mansion at 518 Crestview Drive is a regal French Regency with impressive gates and dual guard houses at the entrance. Surrounded by manicured lawns and topiary-tree box hedges, this 27-room spread has a much-used motor court, a swimming pool, tennis courts, a billiards room and enough bedrooms for all of Ellie Mae's "critters."

Drive up to the front door, step out of Miss Jane Hathaway's Coronet convertible (she trades it in for a red one every year, it seems) and ring the door chimes that Granny and Jethro early on thought were ghosts.

You step down into an oval foyer, complete with built-in pedestal urns, a fleur-de-lis-tiled diamond-patterned floor (perfect for hoe-downs or ballroom dancing) and a sweeping curved staircase that, as a backdrop, makes even Jed's simple duds look runway perfect. Straight ahead is the "parlor" or living room, with "courtin'" couches, a fireplace separating two sets of French doors, and a baby grand piano for visiting cousin Jethrene to play on.

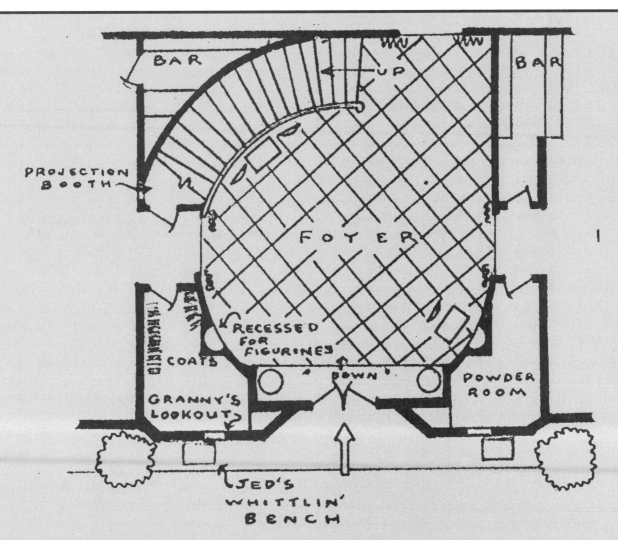

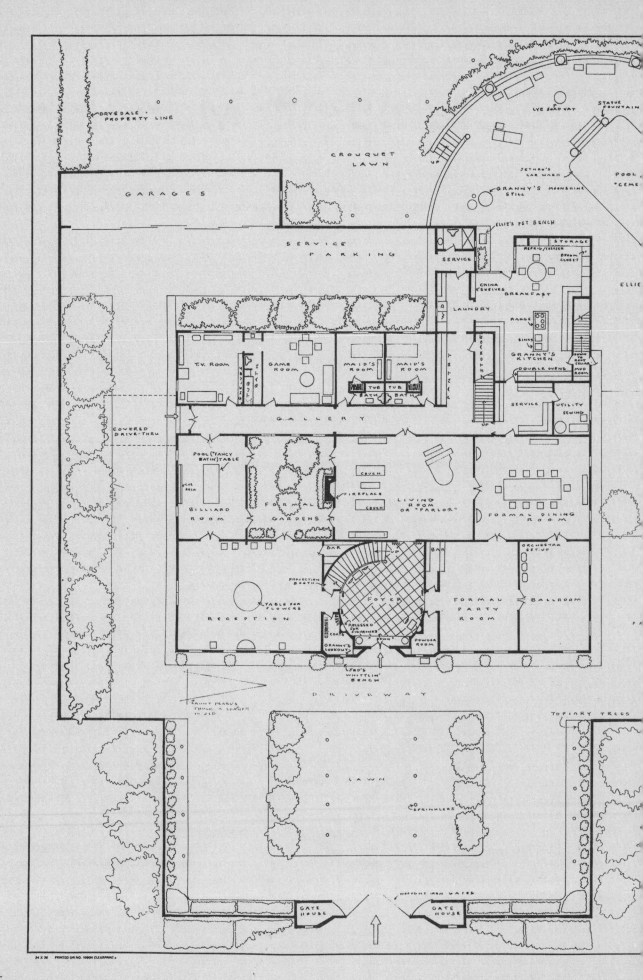

DRYSDALE PROPERTY LINE

CROUQUET LAWN

GARAGES

LYE SOAP VAT

STATUE FOUNTAIN

JETHRO'S CAR WASH

GRANNY'S MOONSHINE STILL

POOL "CEME

SERVICE PARKING

ELLIE'S PET BENCH

STORAGE

SERVICE

REFRIG/FREEZER

BROOM CLOSET

ELLIE

CHINA SHELVES

BREAKFAST

LAUNDRY

RANGE

SINKS

GRANNY'S KITCHEN

DOWN TO ROOT CELLAR

DOUBLE OVENS

MUD ROOM

T.V. ROOM

GAME ROOM

MAID'S ROOM

MAID'S ROOM

BATH

TUB

TUB

BATH

SERVICE

UTILITY

SEWING

GALLERY

COVERED DRIVE-THRU

POOL ("FANCY EATIN") TABLE

CUE RACK

BILLIARD ROOM

FORMAL GARDENS

COUCH

FIREPLACE

COUCH

LIVING ROOM OR "PARLOR"

FORMAL DINING ROOM

BAR

UP

BAR

ORCHESTRA SET-UP

PROJECTION BOOTH

FOYER

FORMAL PARTY ROOM

BALLROOM

TABLE FOR FLOWERS

RECEPTION

COATS

RECESSED FOR FIGURINES

DOWN

POWDER ROOM

GRANNY'S LOOKOUT

JED'S WHITTLIN' BENCH

AUNT PEARL'S TRUCK - A LOANER TO JED

DRIVEWAY

TOPIARY TREES

LAWN

SPRINKLERS

WROUGHT IRON GATES

GATE HOUSE

GATE HOUSE

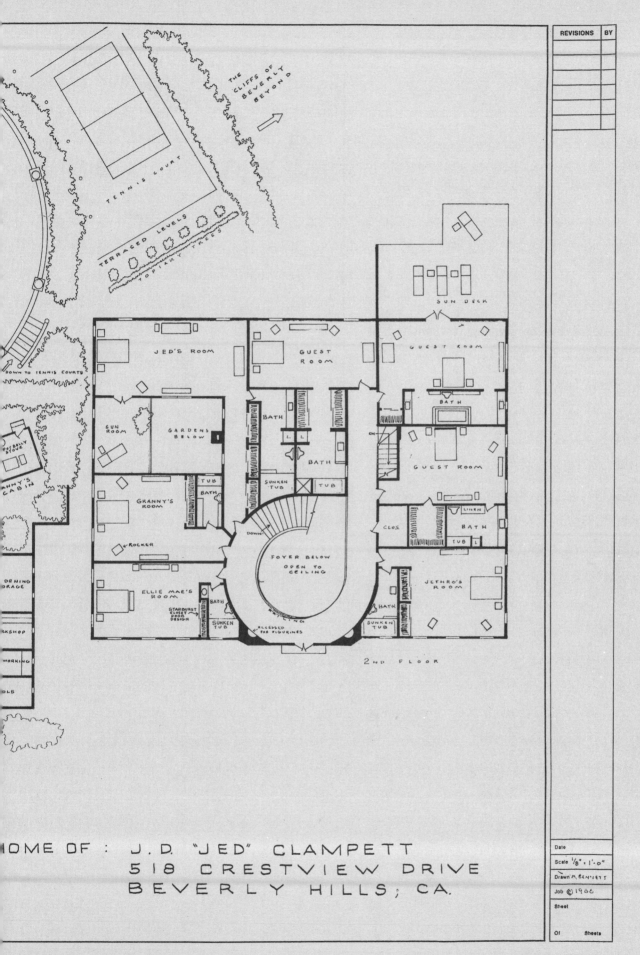

HOME OF : J. D. "JED" CLAMPETT
518 CRESTVIEW DRIVE
BEVERLY HILLS; CA.

"THE BEVERLY HILLBILLIES"

65

The kitchen is a chef's paradise: double ovens, dual range-tops, sub-zero refrigerator/ freezer, a laundry room, and a breakfast nook with seating for four.

Step outside to a glamorous pavilion high above Beverly Hills and check out the swimming pool, with Grecian goddess figurine fountains, an elaborate set of upholstered patio furniture, and Granny's lye soap kettle simmering on a low flame. Enjoy the quiet solitude of this aquatic setting now, before Jethro turns it into a three-minute car wash.

Upstairs, there are countless bedroom suites, all with distinctive starburst-patterned closet doors and elaborate bathrooms (I'm sure with sunken tubs)—all off a circular balcony that sweeps around the foyer.

The Clampetts didn't settle well into their house at first. They ruined the front-lawn sprinkler system once, trying to raise crops. And the sight of Jed whittlin' near the front door would make any casual observer in the neighborhood think the hired help had run amok. No wonder Mrs. Drysdale wanted to move.

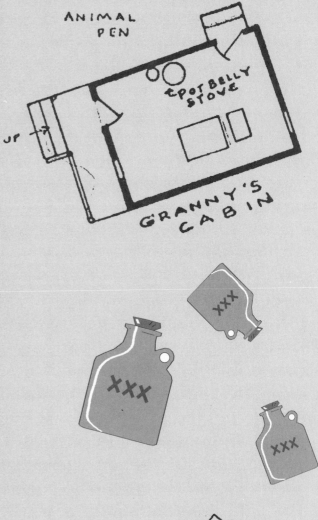

ANIMAL PEN

POTBELLY STOVE

UP →

GRANNY'S CABIN

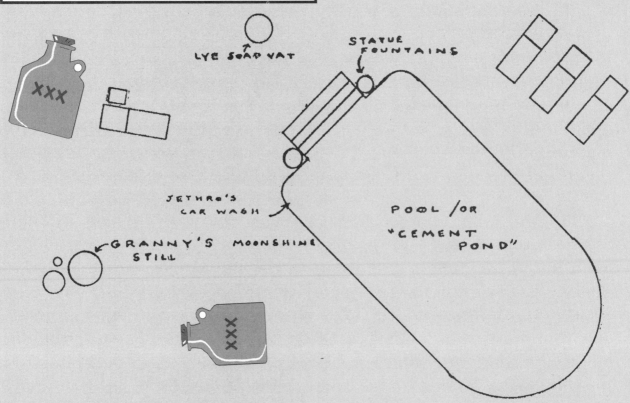

LYE SOAP VAT

STATUE FOUNTAINS

JETHRO'S CAR WASH

GRANNY'S MOONSHINE STILL

POOL /OR "CEMENT POND"

"THE MUNSTERS"

Herman & Lily Munster House

1313 Mockingbird Lane is the home address of Lily and Herman Munster. It's a creepy Victorian with ominous wrought-iron gates and overgrown foliage. Loose shutters, dark, uninviting windows, a massive pair of front doors—this house screams for renovation. No doubt the owners like it this way. These neighbors are no ordinary family. They like the roaring winds, the tumbleweed in the yard, the basement laboratory where Grandpa can try his experiments, the cute little telephone table in the foyer that is actually a coffin.

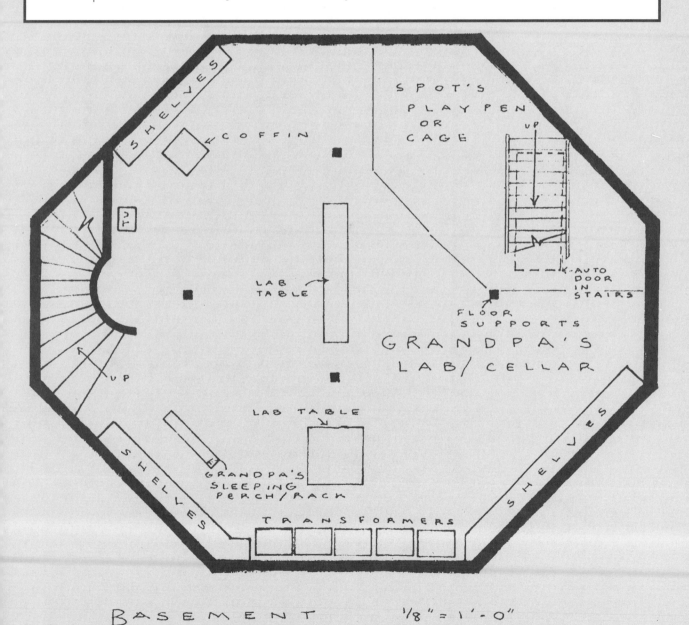

SHELVES

COFFIN

SPOT'S PLAY PEN OR CAGE

UP

LAB TABLE

UP

AUTO DOOR IN STAIRS

FLOOR SUPPORTS

GRANDPA'S LAB / CELLAR

LAB TABLE

SHELVES

GRANDPA'S SLEEPING PERCH / RACK

SHELVES

TRANSFORMERS

BASEMENT   1/8" = 1'-0"

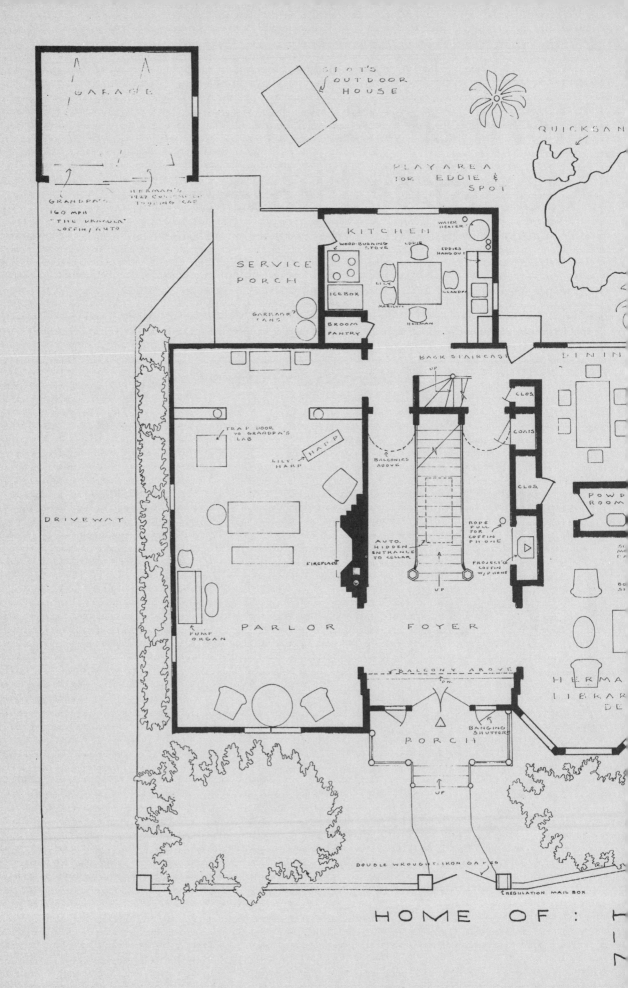

GARAGE

SPOT'S
OUTDOOR
HOUSE

QUICKSAN

PLAY AREA
for EDDIE &
SPOT

GRANDPA'S
160 MPH
"THE DRACULA"
COFFIN/AUTO

HERMAN'S
HOT COMPRESS
TOURING CAR

KITCHEN

WATER
HEATER

SERVICE
PORCH

WOOD-BURNING
STOVE

EDDIE

EDDIES
HANGOUT

LILY

ICEBOX

MARILYN

GRANDPA

GARBAGE
CANS

BROOM
PANTRY

HERMAN

BACK STAIRCASE

DININ

UP

CLOS

TRAP DOOR
TO GRANDPA'S
LAB

HARP

LILY'S
HARP

BALCONIES
ABOVE

COATS

CLOS

DRIVEWAY

POWD
ROOM

ROPE
PULL
FOR
COFFIN
PHONE

AUTO.
HIDDEN
ENTRANCE
TO CELLAR

FIREPLACE

PROJECT'S
COFFIN
W/PHONE

UP

PUMP
ORGAN

PARLOR   FOYER

BALCONY ABOVE

HERMA
LIBRAR
DE

BANGING
SHUTTERS

PORCH

UP

DOUBLE WROUGHT-IRON GATES

REGULATION MAIL BOX

HOME OF : H
N

68

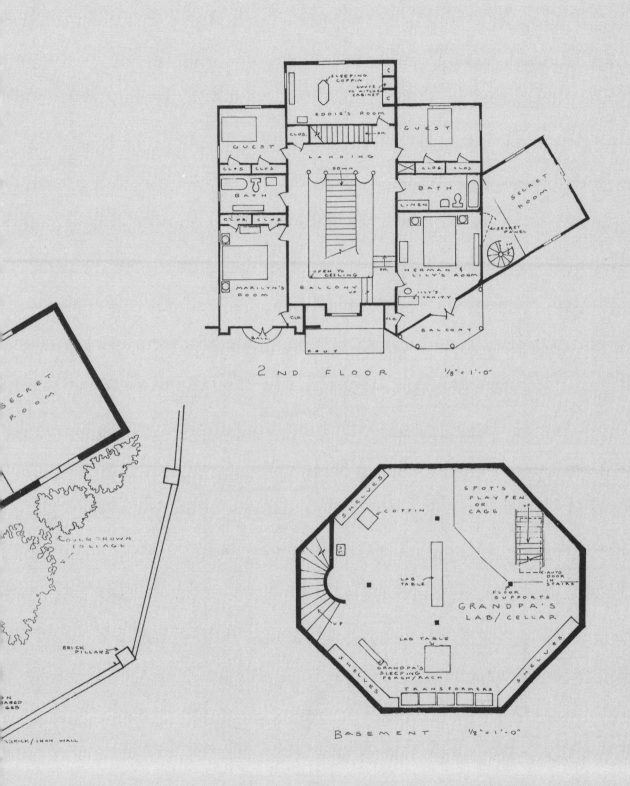

2ND FLOOR   1/8" = 1'-0"

SLEEPING COFFIN

CHUTE TO KITCHEN CABINET

EDDIE'S ROOM

GUEST

CLOS.

GUEST

CL•S CLOS

LANDING

DOWN

BATH

CLOS. CLOS.

SECRET ROOM

SECRET PANEL

BATH

LINEN

OPEN TO CEILING

HERMAN & LILY'S ROOM

MARILYN'S ROOM

BALCONY

LILY'S VANITY

CLO.

CLO.

BALC.

BALCONY

ROOF

SECRET ROOM

OVERGROWN FOLIAGE

BRICK PILLARS

BRICK/IRON WALL

SHELVES

SPOT'S PLAY PEN OR CAGE

COFFIN

LAB TABLE

FLOOR SUPPORTS

AUTO DOOR IN STAIRS

GRANDPA'S LAB/CELLAR

UP

LAB TABLE

GRANDPA'S SLEEPING PERCH/RACK

SHELVES

SHELVES

TRANSFORMERS

BASEMENT   1/8" = 1'-0"

MAN & LILY MUNSTER
MOCKINGBIRD LANE
KINGBIRD HEIGHTS

"THE MUNSTERS"

69

A dramatic main staircase meanders toward the second level and then splits, each side heading down a dark hallway. The furniture is old, musty, covered in spiderwebs. People here sleep in caskets, and children like Eddie Munster dream of being a teen werewolf and have snack time inside kitchen cupboards.

A host of nooks and crannies, with lots of secret doorways and passageways, the Munster home cries out for much-needed repairs and upgrades. Somebody call H.U.D.

QUICKSAND

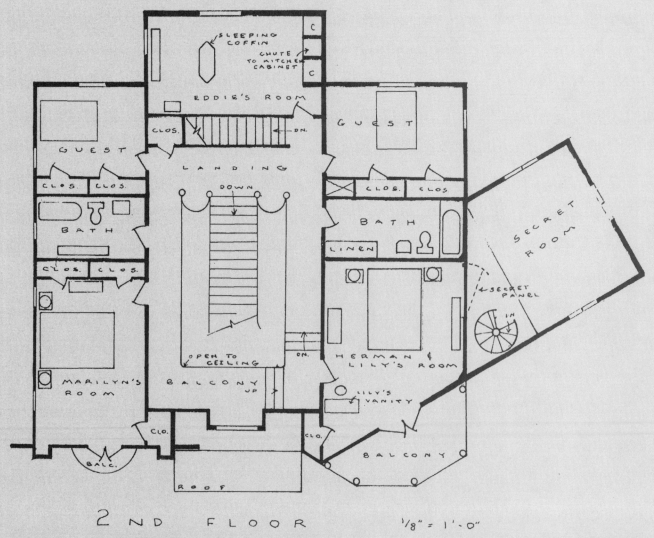

2ND FLOOR   1/8" = 1'-0"

"THE MUNSTERS"

Home of Gomez & Morticia Addams

This old Victorian would scare anyone. Overgrown hedges, tumbleweeds, rusty iron gates, the home of Morticia and Gomez Addams has that Halloween theme all year round.

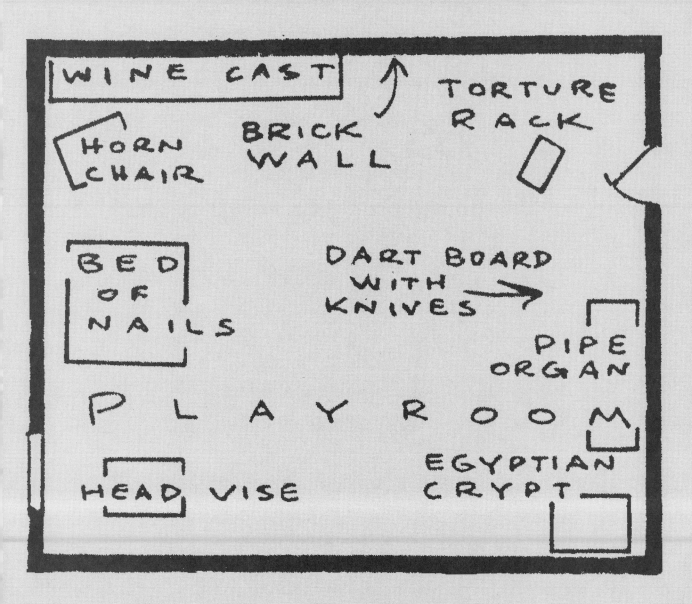

WINE CAST

HORN CHAIR

BRICK WALL

TORTURE RACK

BED OF NAILS

DART BOARD WITH KNIVES

PIPE ORGAN

P L A Y R O O M

HEAD VISE

EGYPTIAN CRYPT

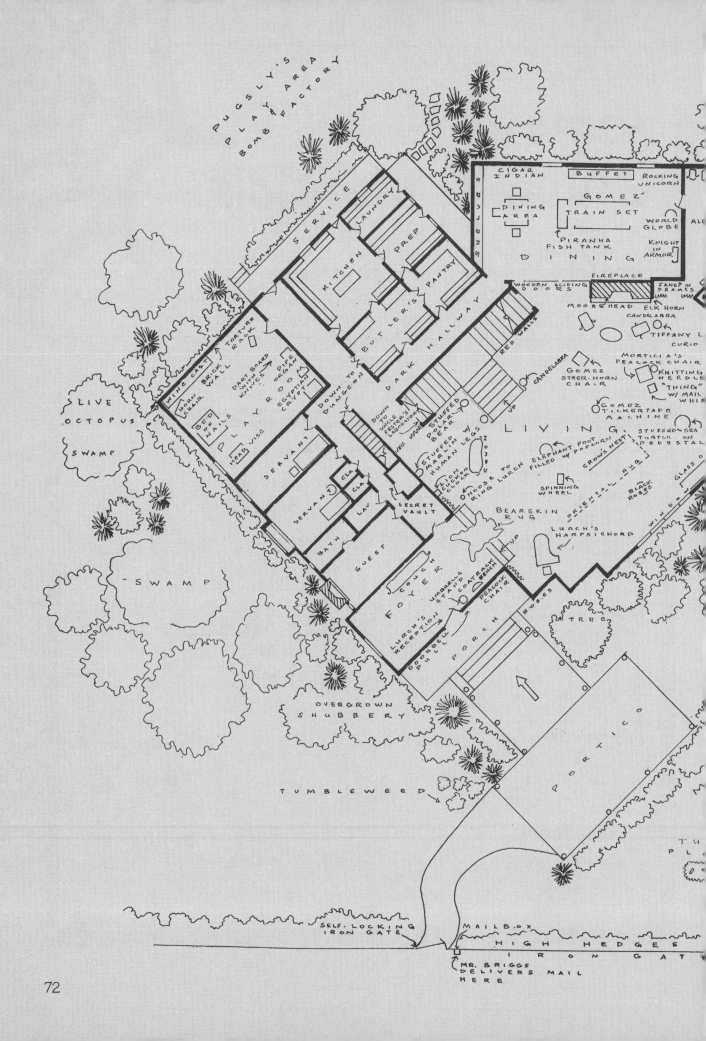

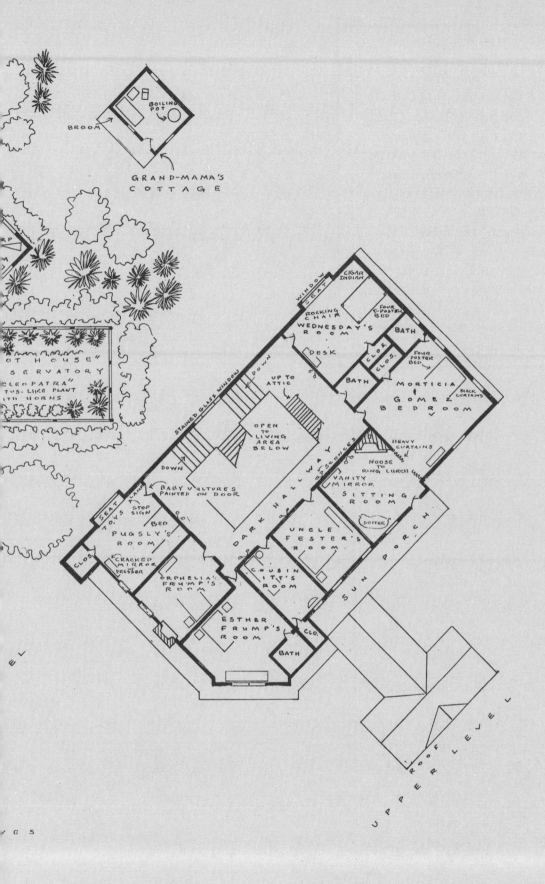

BROOM

BOILING POT

GRAND-MAMA'S COTTAGE

"HOT HOUSE" CONSERVATORY
"CLEOPATRA" CACTUS-LIKE PLANT WITH HORNS

WINDOW SEAT

CIGAR INDIAN

ROCKING CHAIR

WEDNESDAY'S ROOM

FOUR POSTER BED

DESK

BATH

DOWN

UP TO ATTIC

CLO.

CLO.

BATH

FOUR POSTER BED

MORTICIA & GOMEZ BEDROOM

BLACK CURTAINS

STAINED GLASS WINDOW

OPEN TO LIVING AREA BELOW

SCONCES

HEAVY CURTAINS

NOOSE TO RING LURCH

DOWN

VANITY MIRROR

SITTING ROOM

BABY VULTURES PAINTED ON DOOR

SEAT TOYS RAMP

STOP SIGN

BED

PUGSLY'S ROOM

DARK HALLWAY

UNCLE FESTER'S ROOM

SETTEE

CLOS.

CRACKED MIRROR DRESSER

ORPHELIA FRUMP'S ROOM

COUSIN ITT'S ROOM

SUN PORCH

ESTHER FRUMP'S ROOM

CLO.

BATH

ROOF LEVEL

UPPER LEVEL

HOME OF : THE ADDAMS FAMILY

Inside, there are museum-quality furnishings, strange mountings on the walls, and dark heavy velvet curtains drawn over the windows. A host of secret doorways. A foghorn announces the mail delivery. A ticker-tape runs concurrently with the exploding model trains that crash in the dining room. Lerch skulks past, bringing afternoon tea. Uncle Fester likes to stay up late, thinking up mad concoctions in his laboratory. Morticia likes to putter about in her solarium, snipping the buds off blooming roses. A tango is performed by no one in particular while Grandmama makes a yummy eye-of-toad soup.

No wonder Mr. Briggs, the mailman, is seen running from the mailbox every day.

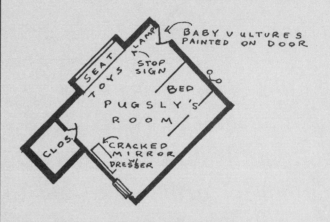

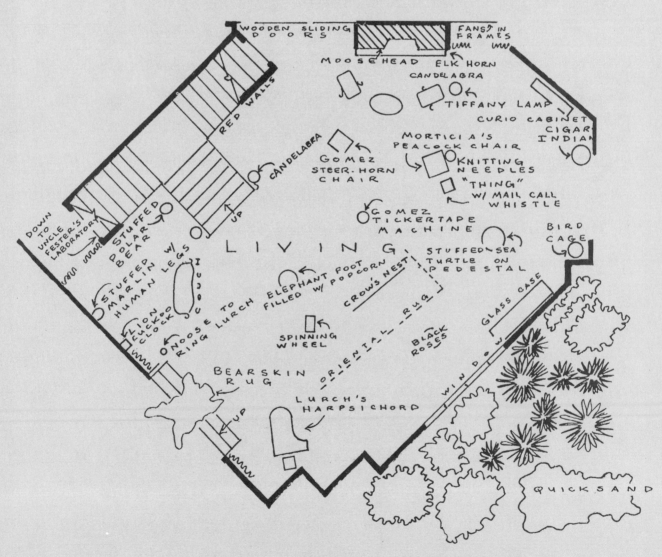

"THE ADDAMS FAMILY"

Rob & Laura Petrie House

Picture a long, low rancher with a prominent bay window and a master bedroom jutting off at a 45-degree angle, and you've got a pretty good idea of what the house at 148 Bonnie Meadow Road looks like. Unfortunately, the Petries were too busy ever to share an exterior view of their home, so we have to imagine a tree-lined, sidewalked street of well-appointed homes in a better part of Westchester County. Rumor has it that the Helpers, Millie and Jerry, first looked at the Petrie house to buy, but passed on it after discovering a giant rock, complete with bubbling spring, in the basement.

We must hand it to the Petries. From the built-in planters to the grass-cloth wallpaper, Rob and Laura decorate with the best of them—and on one income. Not everyone could turn this dramatic angular sunken living-room into such an inviting entertainment pad. Is it all those silk pillows arranged neatly on the window seat that makes us want to move in? Or is it the tasteful easy chair with ottoman (the one that Rob always trips over) by the front door? Or the Swedish fireplace on a half-moon, used-brick hearth—and with a built-in loveseat, no less?

The kitchen is sleek, with clean lines. An island range rests at an angle to form a galley kitchen in the center of the room while the built-in oven and refrigerator stand in the background behind the double swinging door to the dining area. A glass-shelved china shelf separates the breakfast area from the service entrance where Millie usually makes her morning battle cry. Knoll table and chairs complete an efficient breakfast area. There are personal touches like the bread-box and toaster, and there are plenty

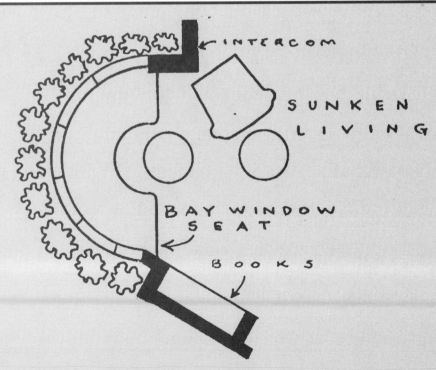

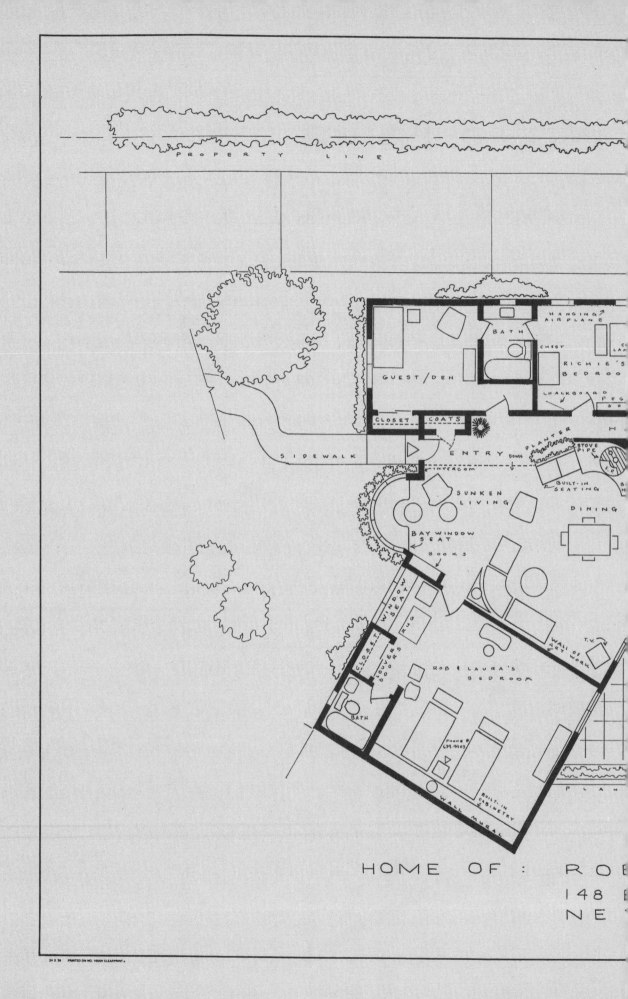

PROPERTY LINE

GUEST/DEN

BATH

HANGING AIRPLANE

CHEST

RICHIE'S BEDROOM

CHALKBOARD

PEG SH

CLOSET

COATS

SIDEWALK

ENTRY

DOWN

INTERCOM

PLANTER

STOVE PIPE

H

BUILT-IN SEATING

SUNKEN LIVING

DINING

BAY WINDOW SEAT

BOOKS

WINDOW SEAT

RUG

CLOSET

LOUVERS DOORS

ROB & LAURA'S BEDROOM

WALL OF ART WORK

T.V.

BATH

PHONE # 699-9405

WALL MURAL

BUILT-IN CABINETRY

PLAN

HOME OF : ROB

148 B

NE

24 X 36   PRINTED ON NO. 1000H CLEARPRINT ⊕

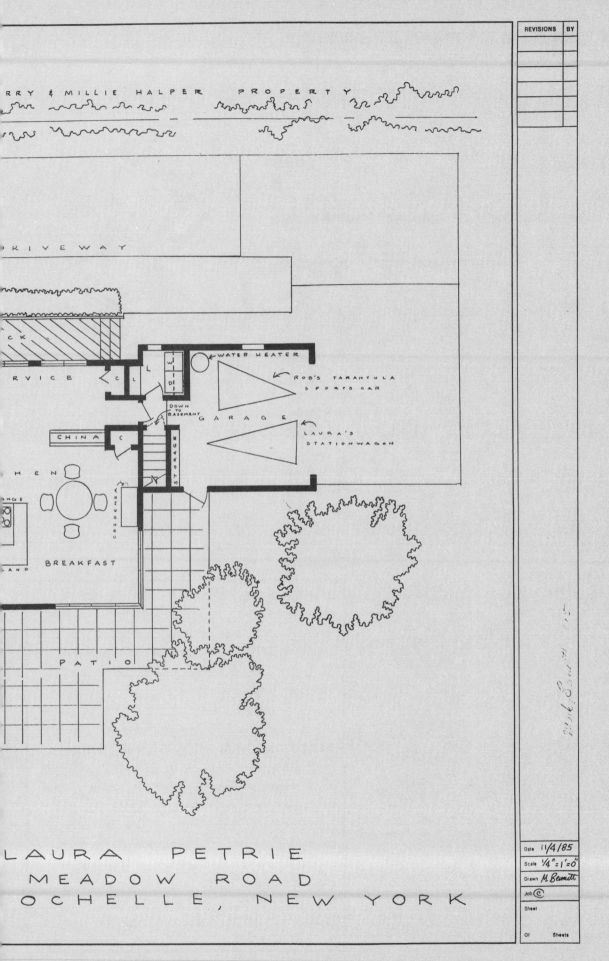

RRY & MILLIE HALPER PROPERTY

DRIVEWAY

WATER HEATER

ROB'S TARANTULA
SPORTS CAR

SERVICE < CL

DOWN
TO
BASEMENT

GARAGE

LAURA'S
STATIONWAGON

CHINA C

BREAKFAST

STORAGE

PATIO

LAURA PETRIE
MEADOW ROAD
OCHELLE, NEW YORK

REVISIONS | BY

Date 11/4/85
Scale ¼"=1'=0"
Drawn M. Bennett
Job C
Sheet
OI   Sheets

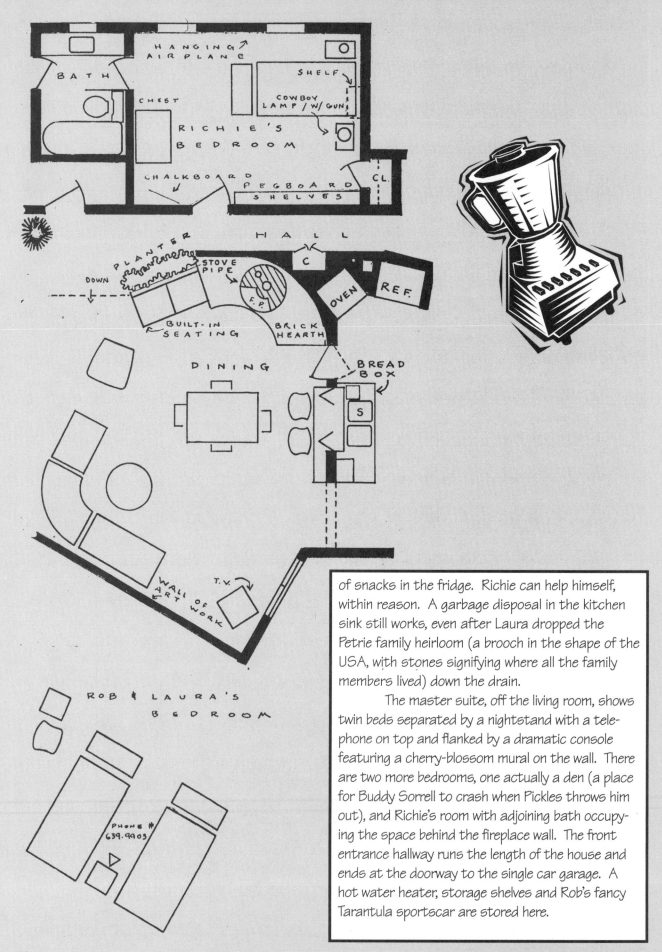

BATH

HANGING AIRPLANE

SHELF

CHEST

COWBOY LAMP / W/ GUN

RICHIE'S BEDROOM

CHALKBOARD

PEGBOARD SHELVES

CL.

PLANTER

HALL

C

STOVE PIPE

DOWN

F.P.

OVEN

REF.

BUILT-IN SEATING

BRICK HEARTH

BREAD BOX

DINING

S

WALL OF ART WORK

T.V.

ROB & LAURA'S BEDROOM

PHONE # 639.9903

of snacks in the fridge. Richie can help himself, within reason. A garbage disposal in the kitchen sink still works, even after Laura dropped the Petrie family heirloom (a brooch in the shape of the USA, with stones signifying where all the family members lived) down the drain.

The master suite, off the living room, shows twin beds separated by a nightstand with a telephone on top and flanked by a dramatic console featuring a cherry-blossom mural on the wall. There are two more bedrooms, one actually a den (a place for Buddy Sorrell to crash when Pickles throws him out), and Richie's room with adjoining bath occupying the space behind the fireplace wall. The front entrance hallway runs the length of the house and ends at the doorway to the single car garage. A hot water heater, storage shelves and Rob's fancy Tarantula sportscar are stored here.

"THE DICK VAN DYKE SHOW"

"BEWITCHED"

Darrin & Samantha Stevens House

The home of Darrin and Samantha Stevens at 1164 Morning Glory Circle, in Patterson, New York, is a quaint Dutch Colonial built in the early 1960s. From the first time Samantha and Endora twitched their magical powers to produce plants, shrubbery, awnings and furniture, the Stevens home has always been a quality residence of good taste.

A two-level home of brick and wood, this gabled steep-roofed structure consists of an open living and dining room, surrounding a prominent staircase near the foyer. A raised brick hearth and fireplace is a focal point of the living room as are the three sets of French doors out to the patio in back.

The dining area also features a bay window with built-in seat cushions, a louver-shuttered pass-through, a Grecian mural panel, and fully stocked bar (martinis a specialty of the house). Through a double swinging service door,

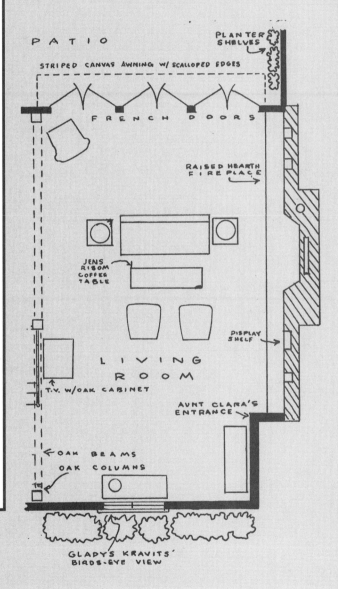

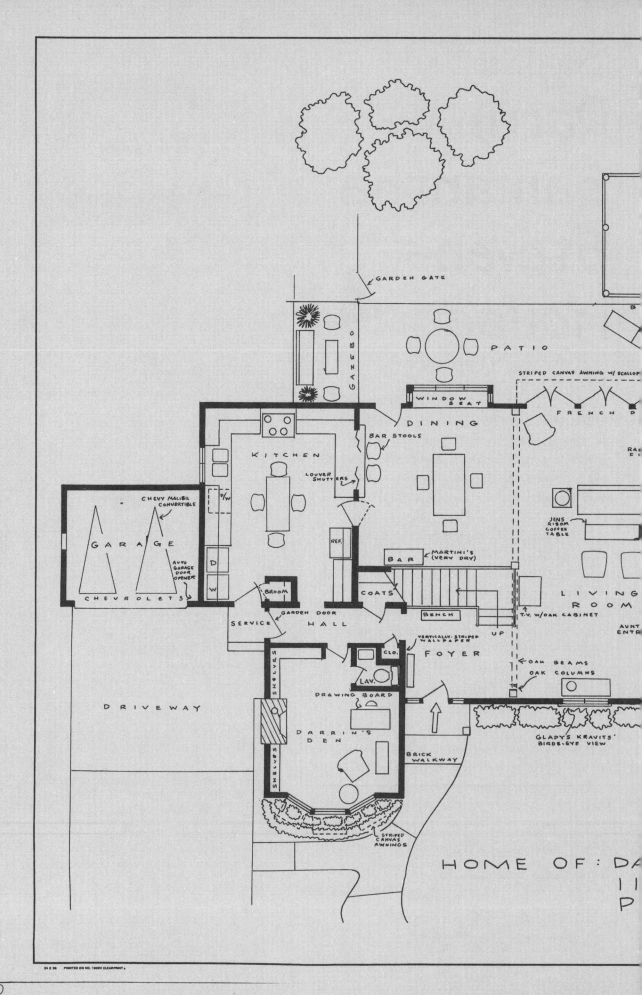

GARDEN GATE

GAZEBO

PATIO

STRIPED CANVAS AWNING w/ SCALLOP

WINDOW SEAT

DINING

FRENCH D

BAR STOOLS

KITCHEN

LOUVER SHUTTERS

RA
F

CHEVY MALIBU CONVERTIBLE

D/W

JENS RISOM COFFEE TABLE

GARAGE

REF.

AUTO GARAGE DOOR OPENER

D

BAR

MARTINI'S (VERY DRY)

CHEVROLETS

W

BROOM

COATS

LIVING ROOM

GARDEN DOOR

BENCH

T.V. w/OAK CABINET

SERVICE

HALL

UP

AVNT
ENTR

VERTICALLY-STRIPED WALLPAPER

CLO.

FOYER

OAK BEAMS

SHELVES

LAV.

OAK COLUMNS

DRIVEWAY

DRAWING BOARD

DARRIN'S DEN

BRICK WALKWAY

GLADYS KRAVITS' BIRDS-EYE VIEW

SHELVES

STRIPED CANVAS AWNINGS

HOME OF: DA
11
P

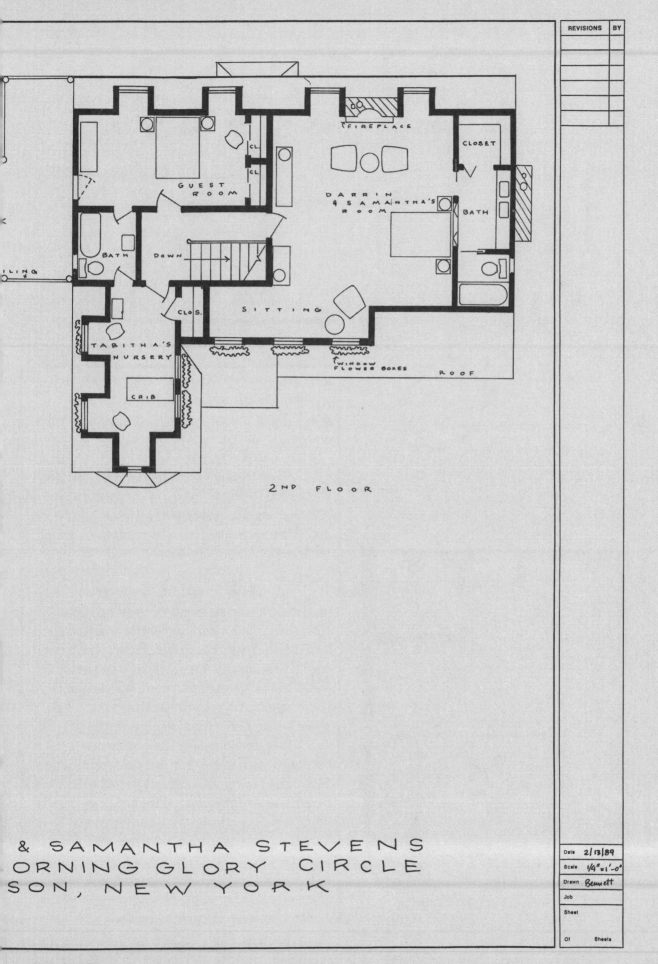

GUEST ROOM

CL.

CL.

FIREPLACE

CLOSET

DARRIN & SAMANTHA'S ROOM

BATH

BATH

DOWN

CLOS.

SITTING

TABITHA'S NURSERY

CRIB

WINDOW FLOWER BOXES

ROOF

2ND FLOOR

& SAMANTHA STEVENS
ORNING GLORY CIRCLE
SON, NEW YORK

REVISIONS	BY

Date	2/13/89
Scale	1/4"=1'-0"
Drawn	Bennett
Job	
Sheet	
Of	Sheets

"BEWITCHED"

TABITHA'S NURSERY

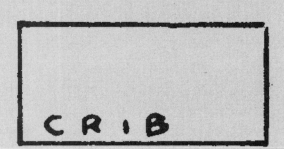

CRIB

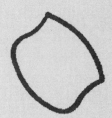

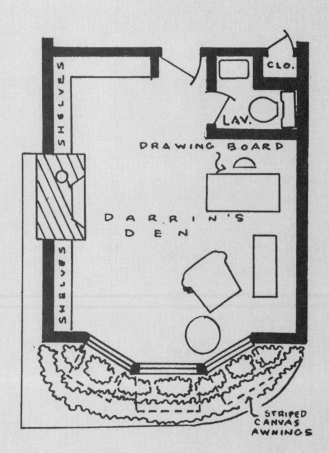

SHELVES

SHELVES

CLO.

LAV.

DRAWING BOARD

DARRIN'S DEN

STRIPED CANVAS AWNINGS

a modern kitchen offers a washer and dryer, a dishwasher, a range and oven (for baked Alaska) and a broom closet. A breakfast table and four chairs are in the center of this room.

Darrin's den has the large bay window at the front of the house. A fireplace and bookshelves are against one wall, a couch and drawing board near the window. A small bathroom is near the door.

A hallway leads from the foyer to a garden door and service porch and garage outside, Here, Darrin and Samantha keep their late-model Chevrolets inside the automatically-opening garage. Upstairs, there is a master suite, complete with bathroom, dressing area and cozy fireplace. Darrin and Samantha's bed rests under a shuttered window off the dressing room. Two low dormer windows offer a view outside. There is another bedroom, eventually Tabitha's nursery, and a guest room for Darrin's parents when they visit.

In general, furnishings are high-end and modern. Jens Risom coffee-table, a four cushioned couch, a Hans Wenger papa bear chair with ottoman, mixed with provincial Windsor chairs. Decorator-perfect.

"BEWITCHED"

"THE BRADY BUNCH"
Mike & Carol Brady House

This split-level contemporary, located at 4222 Clinton Way in Los Angeles, features three bedrooms, three bathrooms and a maid's room for Alice. A double-door entry leads to a dramatic cathedral-ceilinged living/dining room, where Mike and Carol entertain guests and occasionally conduct parent-child powwows. Mike's den is separated from the living room by a brick fireplace and adjustable louver shutters—permanently closed when Greg temporarily makes it into his "crash pad."

The kitchen is an ideal workplace for the two cooks, Carol and Alice, who often work together to prepare meals. Done in birch cabinetry and orange formica countertops, the kitchen features a dishwasher, refrigerator/freezer, double ovens and an indoor barbecue grill. A cozy den behind the serving counter houses the family entertainment center: hi-fi, color television, game table. Alice's room, near the laundry room/service porch, contains louver-door closets and an adjoining bath.

A slate patio runs the width of the house and is accessible through sliding doors. A detached double carport which stores the Bradys' Plymouth autos (Mike's sporty convertible and Carol's sensible station wagon) sits at the back of the property, along with a children's play area and Tiger's doghouse.

The second floor, reached by the distinctive cantilevered staircase, boasts two children's rooms, with a shared bath, and a master suite with dressing area and bath. There is a stairway up to a roomy attic, which later becomes a bedroom as first Greg, then Marcia, grow into their teens.

TIGER'S DOG HOUSE

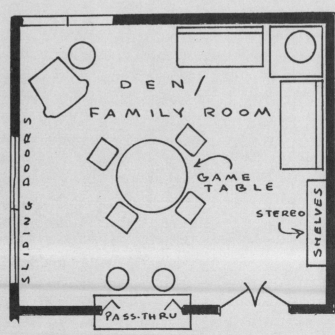

DEN / FAMILY ROOM

SLIDING DOORS

GAME TABLE

STEREO

SHELVES

PASS-THRU

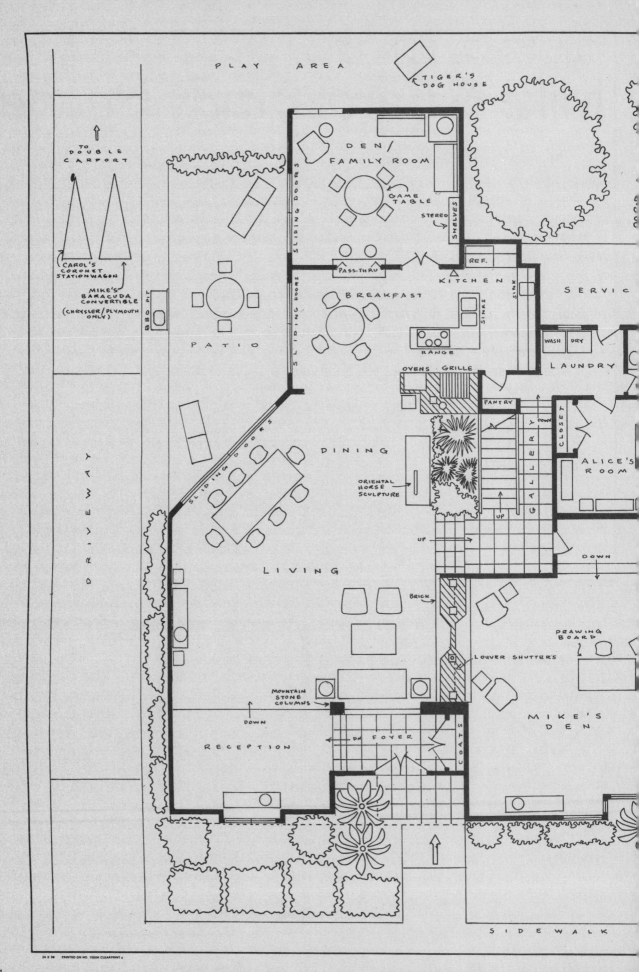

PLAY AREA

TIGER'S DOG HOUSE

DEN/ FAMILY ROOM

GAME TABLE

STEREO

SHELVES

PASS-THRU

REF.

KITCHEN

SERVIC

BREAKFAST

SINKS

RANGE

WASH DRY

LAUNDRY

TO DOUBLE CARPORT

CAROL'S CORONET STATION WAGON

MIKE'S BARACUDA CONVERTIBLE (CHRYSLER / PLYMOUTH ONLY)

BBQ PIT

PATIO

SLIDING DOORS

SLIDING DOORS

OVENS GRILLE

PANTRY

GALLERY

CLOSET

DINING

ORIENTAL HORSE SCULPTURE

ALICE'S ROOM

DRIVEWAY

SLIDING DOORS

UP

UP

DOWN

LIVING

BRICK

DRAWING BOARD

LOUVER SHUTTERS

MIKE'S DEN

MOUNTAIN STONE COLUMNS

DOWN

RECEPTION

DN FOYER

COATS

SIDEWALK

24 X 36 PRINTED ON NO. 1000H CLEARPRINT

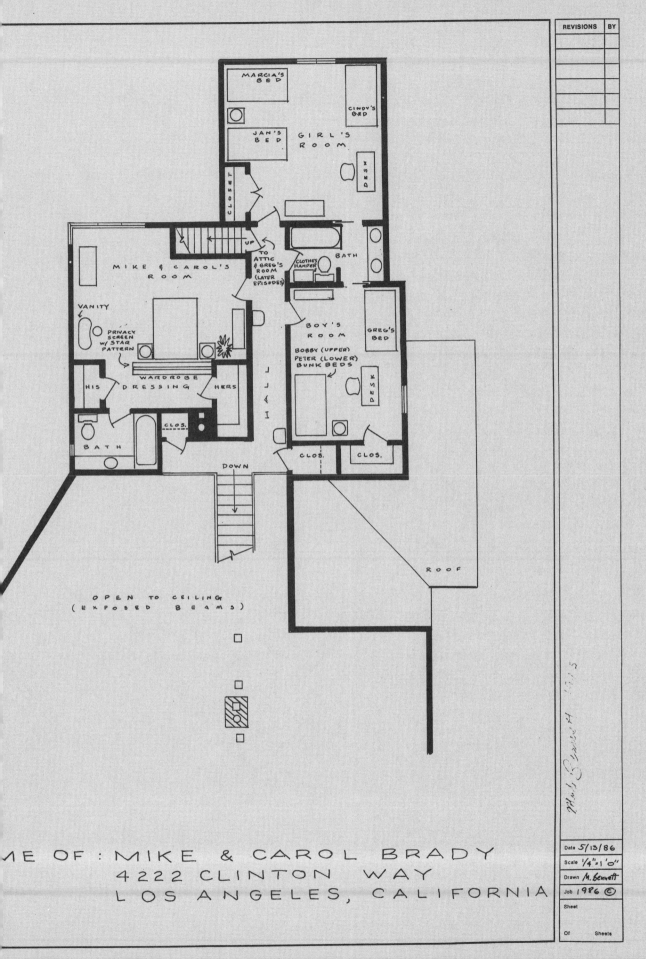

MARCIA'S BED

CINDY'S BED

JAN'S BED

GIRL'S ROOM

DESK

CLOSET

MIKE & CAROL'S ROOM

UP

TO ATTIC & GREG'S ROOM (LATER EPISODES)

CLOTHES HAMPER

BATH

VANITY

PRIVACY SCREEN w/ STAR PATTERN

BOY'S ROOM

GREG'S BED

BOBBY (UPPER) PETER (LOWER) BUNK BEDS

DESK

WARDROBE

HIS   DRESSING   HERS

CLOS.

BATH

CLOS.

CLOS.

DOWN

CLOS.

OPEN TO CEILING
(EXPOSED BEAMS)

ROOF

REVISIONS | BY

Date 5/13/86
Scale 1/4"=1'0"
Drawn M. Bennett
Job 1986 ©
Sheet
Of   Sheets

ME OF: MIKE & CAROL BRADY
4222 CLINTON WAY
LOS ANGELES, CALIFORNIA

"THE BRADY BUNCH"

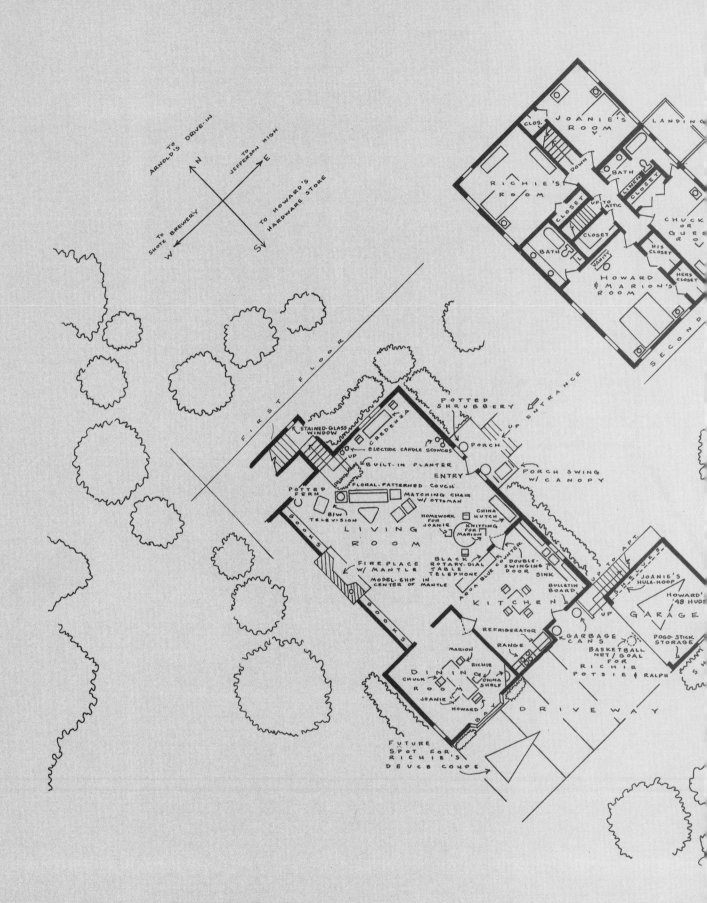

"HAPPY DAYS"

Home of the Cunninghams

Howard and Marion Cunningham are wonderful parents. They have made a comfortable home for their three children: Chuck, who is away at college; Richie, a star high-school student; and Joanie, a junior-high darling. The Cunningham house is also the local favorite hangout for Richie's friends.

Enter the home from the front porch, past the potted topiary shrubbery and canopied porch swing, and you will find an open living room with dining table (the perfect place to do homework), a large fireplace with a model ship on the mantle, a built-in planter by the staircase and a set of vibrant, modern-print curtains with sheers and venetian blinds on the windows. Wall sconces give the room a warm hue.

The kitchen is updated, with a counter separating the living area from the linoleum-floored breakfast area. There is a black table-model telephone on the pass-through. A service door leads out to the garage with a basketball goal set up, regulation-height. Fonzie, the local ex-juvenile-delinquent and leather-clad mechanic, rents the room above the garage.

The house is close to Howard's hardware store and Arnold's Drive-In. Schott's Brewery is all the way across town.

ROOF

BATH

CUPBOARD
HOT PLATE

DARTBOARD
ON DOOR

BIN PHOTO'S

KIT.

REF.

SOFA BED

HI-FI

COAT RACK w/ MIRROR

CLO.

JAMES DEAN POSTER ON DOOR

TABLE

FONZIE'S GARAGE APT.

HUTCH

DOWN

UPPER LEVEL

GARAGE APT.

HOME OF: THE CUNNINGHAMS
MILWAUKEE, WISCONSIN

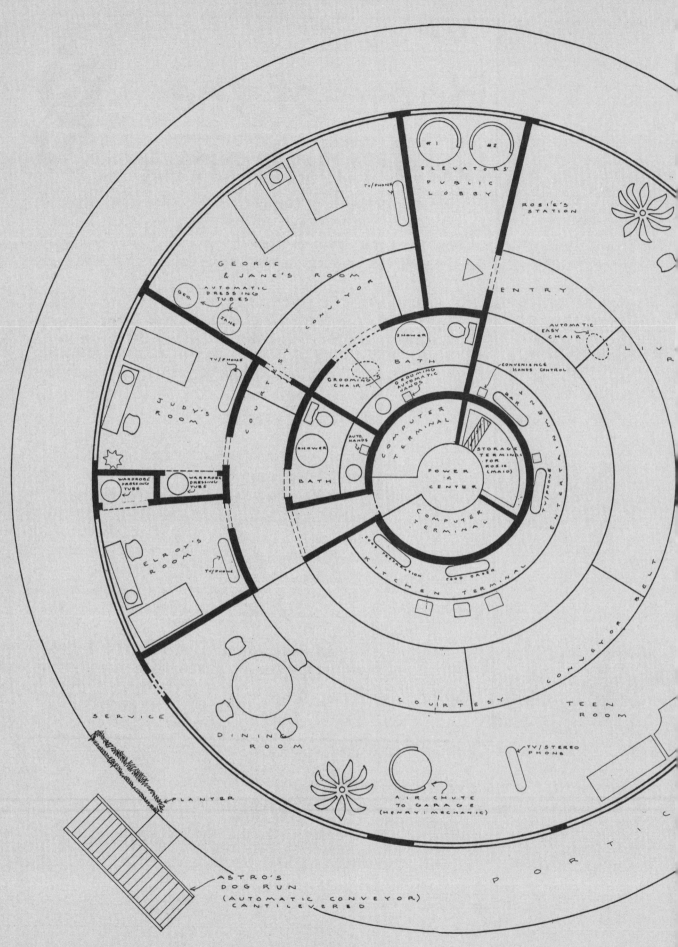

ELEVATORS
#1   #2
PUBLIC LOBBY
TV/PHONE
ROSIE'S STATION
ENTRY
GEORGE & JANE'S ROOM
AUTOMATIC DRESSING TUBES
GEO.
JANE
CONVEYOR
SHOWER
BATH
AUTOMATIC EASY CHAIR
LIV
TV/PHONE
GROOMING CHAIR
GROOMING AUTOMATIC HANDS
CONVENIENCE HANDS CONTROL
BAR
NEW
JUDY'S ROOM
SHOWER
AUTO. HANDS
COMPUTER TERMINAL
STORAGE TERMINAL FOR ROSIE (MAID)
COURTESY
BATH
POWER CENTER
ENTERTAIN
TV/PHONE
WARDROBE DRESSING TUBE
WARDROBE DRESSING TUBE
COMPUTER TERMINAL
ELROY'S ROOM
TV/PHONE
FOOD PREPARATION
FOOD ORDER
KITCHEN TERMINAL
COURTESY
CONVEYOR BELT
TEEN ROOM
SERVICE
DINING ROOM
TV/STEREO PHONE
PLANTER
AIR CHUTE TO GARAGE (HENRY: MECHANIC)
PORT
ASTRO'S DOG RUN (AUTOMATIC CONVEYOR) CANTILEVERED

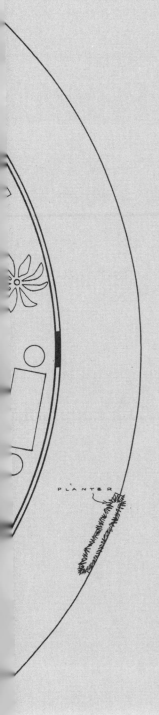

PLANTER

"THE JETSONS"
Home of the Jetsons

Hello. How would you like living in the clouds in this swank unit in the round?

An elevator tube whisks you up into the home of George and Jane Jetson. The front door is a panel that slides up and down automatically. Rosie, the maid, takes your hat as you are conveyor-belted down a circular path, eyeing the stark living room, Judy's teen room, and a computerized food-prep-and-communications station at the core of the apartment, where any food can be presented at the push of a button. There are three bedrooms, with automatic wardrobe changing tubes, large-screen television/telephones that descend from the ceiling in all rooms, and, of course, walls of glass that look out on (what else?) the galaxy.

HOME OF: THE JETSONS
GEORGE, JANE, JUDY, ELROY & ASTRO

The apartment house garage is on the lower level. You can be transported in a matter of seconds via a clear service tube by the den. Everything from schools to shopping centers to Spacely Sprockets is just a helioport away.

Now if we could just teach Astro to walk himself on that cantilevered dog run.

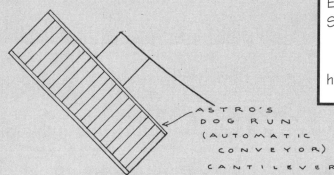

ASTRO'S
DOG RUN
(AUTOMATIC
CONVEYOR)
CANTILEVERED

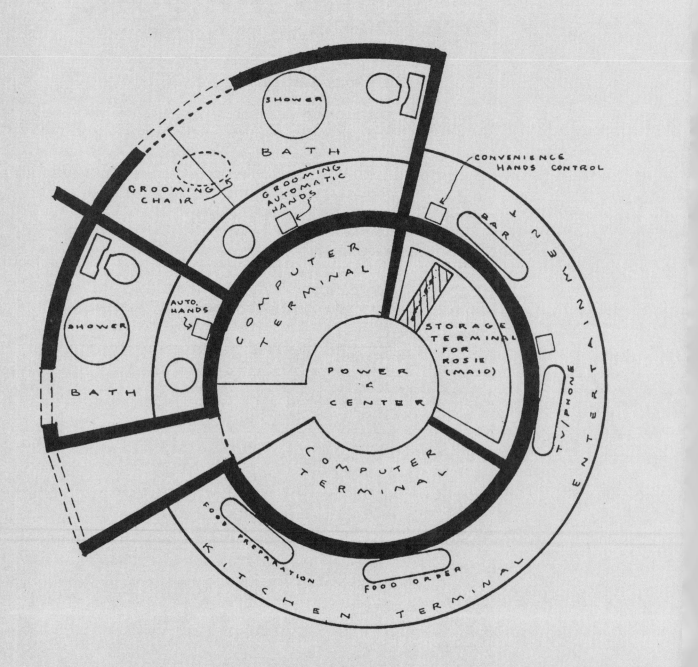

SHOWER

BATH

GROOMING
CHAIR

GROOMING
AUTOMATIC
HANDS

CONVENIENCE
HANDS CONTROL

BAR

ENTERTAINMENT

COMPUTER
TERMINAL

STORAGE
TERMINAL
FOR
ROSIE
(MA10)

AUTO.
HANDS

SHOWER

POWER
&
CENTER

TV/PHONE

BATH

COMPUTER
TERMINAL

FOOD
PREPARATION

FOOD ORDER

KITCHEN TERMINAL

"THE JETSONS"

"THE HONEYMOONERS"

Home of Ralph & Alice Kramden

In a two-room flat in the Bensonhurst section of Brooklyn live Ralph and Alice Kramden, a city bus driver and his wife.

These Kramdens—they are a no-nonsense couple who decorate on a budget. In the main room—a simple round table and chairs, a dresser (probably borrowed from Alice's mother), a candy dish. This apartment is basic with a capital 'B.' There is a view of the city off the fire escape.

No kids trick-or-treat here.

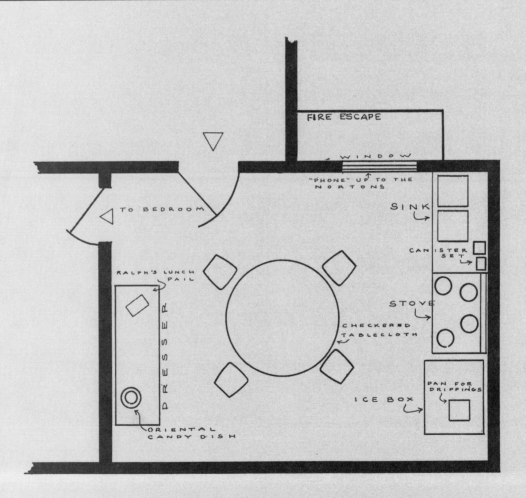

HOME OF: RALPH & ALICE KRAMDEN
328 CHAUNCEY STREET
BENSONHURST
BROOKLYN, NEW YORK

"THE FLINTSTONES"

Home of Fred & Wilma Flintstone

In the town of Bedrock, hard by the rock quarry, is the home of Fred and Wilma Flintstone. It's a nice place, really. An occasional palm tree is budding in the yard, enclosed within a rock wall.

A flat-top roof affair, the Flintstone house has that organic touch. Free-form walls, open living spaces and round windows—you get the feeling that Fred and Wilma are nature types. There are arched doorways. The furniture blends in nicely with the environment. Slab couches of granite, lamp shades of yak skin, an elephant tusk for a phone receiver—these Flintstones carry the caveman theme throughout.

Notice that the kitchen offers a bit of a primitive aspect. A large warthog under the sink is the garbage disposal. An elephant out the kitchen window doubles as the dishwasher and the showerhead. A cuckoo bird serves as the cuckoo clock. Only Dino, the family pet, is not a working appliance. He even gets to go to the drive-in with the family, but he does have to help pedal.

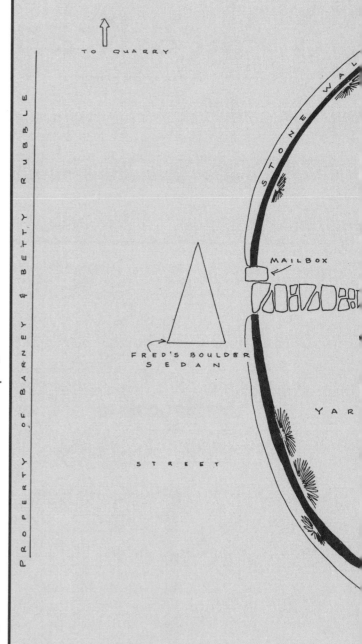

TO QUARRY

PROPERTY OF BARNEY & BETTY RUBBLE

STONE WALL

MAILBOX

FRED'S BOULDER SEDAN

YAR

STREET

TO ROCK VEGAS

TO DRIVE-IN MOVIE & RESTAURANT

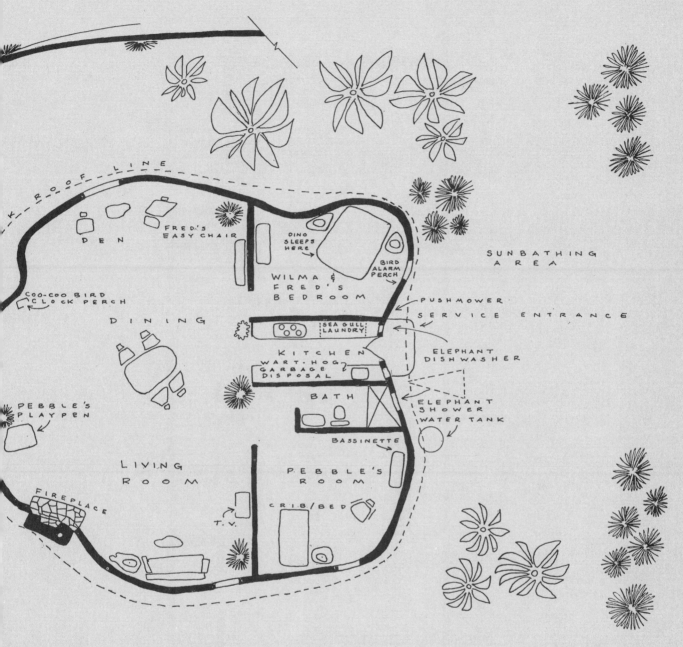

DEN

FRED'S EASY CHAIR

ROOF LINE

COO-COO BIRD CLOCK PERCH

DINING

DINO SLEEPS HERE

WILMA & FRED'S BEDROOM

BIRD ALARM PERCH

SUNBATHING AREA

PUSHMOWER SERVICE ENTRANCE

SEA GULL LAUNDRY

KITCHEN

WART-HOG GARBAGE DISPOSAL

ELEPHANT DISHWASHER

PEBBLE'S PLAYPEN

BATH

ELEPHANT SHOWER WATER TANK

BASSINETTE

LIVING ROOM

PEBBLE'S ROOM

FIREPLACE

T.V.

CRIB/BED

HOME OF FRED & WILMA FLINTSTONE
BEDROCK, U.S.A.

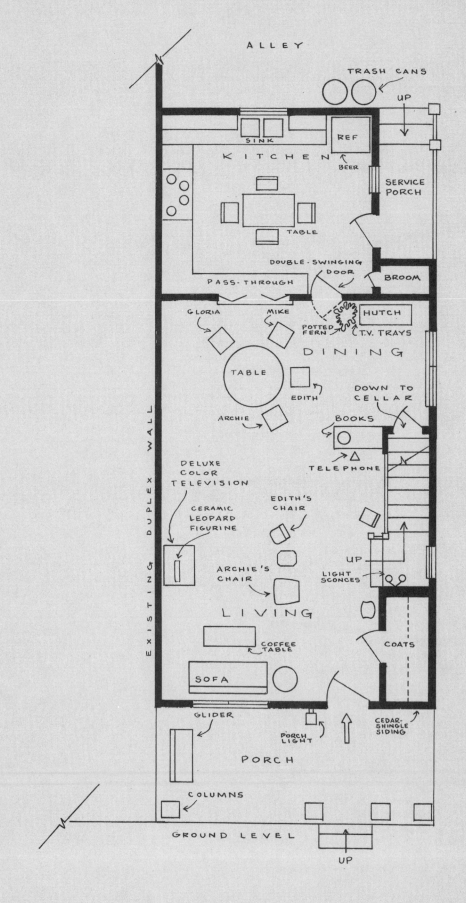

ALLEY

TRASH CANS

UP

SINK

KITCHEN

REF

BEER

SERVICE
PORCH

TABLE

DOUBLE-SWINGING
DOOR

BROOM

PASS-THROUGH

GLORIA

MIKE

HUTCH

POTTED
FERN

T.V. TRAYS

DINING

TABLE

EDITH

DOWN TO
CELLAR

ARCHIE

BOOKS

TELEPHONE

DELUXE
COLOR
TELEVISION

CERAMIC
LEOPARD
FIGURINE

EDITH'S
CHAIR

UP

ARCHIE'S
CHAIR

LIGHT
SCONCES

LIVING

COATS

COFFEE
TABLE

SOFA

GLIDER

PORCH
LIGHT

CEDAR-
SHINGLE
SIDING

PORCH

COLUMNS

GROUND LEVEL

UP

EXISTING DUPLEX WALL

HOME O

"ALL IN THE FAMILY"

Home of Archie & Edith Bunker

Deep in the borough of Queens, New York, in an attached row house, live Edith and Archie Bunker and Mike and Gloria Stivic.

A two-story structure, with a cellar, the Bunker house sits in a racially-mixed neighborhood. Inside, there are easy chairs and a couch in need of upholstering and a large dining-table with seating for six. There is a pass-through between the kitchen and dining areas (kept closed) and a double swinging kitchen door.

The kitchen is basic, with broom closet, a service porch, a stove and double kitchen sinks. There is no dishwasher. Ice-cold beer is in the refrigerator.

Upstairs, there are two bedrooms, each with a closet, and one bathroom with a noisy toilet.

CHEST

CLOSET

ARCHIE & EDITH'S BEDROOM

DRESSING TABLE

DRESSER

CLOSET

DOWN

LINEN

HALL

TH

S

OSET

DRESSER

MIKE & GLORIA'S BEDROOM

LOTS OF PHILOSOPHY BOOKS / TEXTBOOKS SHELVES

ROOF

ND FLOOR

PROPERTY LINE : GEORGE & LOUISE JEFFERSON

CHIE & EDITH BUNKER

4 HOUSER

EENS, NEW YORK

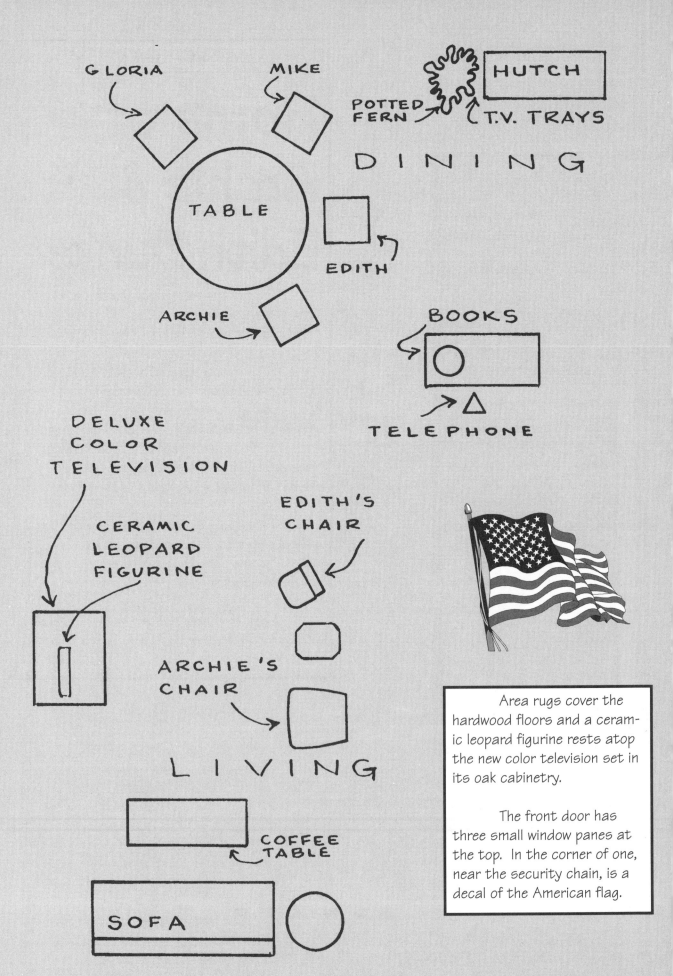

GLORIA

MIKE

POTTED FERN

HUTCH

T.V. TRAYS

D I N I N G

TABLE

EDITH

ARCHIE

BOOKS

TELEPHONE

DELUXE COLOR TELEVISION

CERAMIC LEOPARD FIGURINE

EDITH'S CHAIR

ARCHIE'S CHAIR

L I V I N G

COFFEE TABLE

SOFA

Area rugs cover the hardwood floors and a ceramic leopard figurine rests atop the new color television set in its oak cabinetry.

The front door has three small window panes at the top. In the corner of one, near the security chain, is a decal of the American flag.

"ALL IN THE FAMILY"

"MY THREE SONS"

Steven Douglas Bryant Park House

The Steven Douglas house in Bryant Park is a two-story Colonial with white wood siding and two sets of double bay windows. A red brick walkway leads the visitor up a terraced yard, with appropriate shrubbery, to a columned porch and a single front door, a panel of glass on either side. A gold-plated mail slot and door-knocker complete the picture.

Inside, a living room is to the left and features a bookshelf partition with column for the telephone—a good backdrop for Steve's leather easy chair with ottoman. A sofa and coffee-table face the fireplace and a console television.

A dining room with Queen Anne chairs is to the right of the foyer. Chair-railing is prominent throughout this room. Beyond the second-floor staircase, through a double swinging kitchen door, is where the real action takes place. Bub, the *hausfrau* and uncle to Mike, Robbie and Chip, dishes up hot meals for the centrally-located breakfast table with revolving lazy Susan. A bulletin board is prominent above the table, a place to jot down important notes about stuff like track practice or a favorite recipe clipped from the local paper.

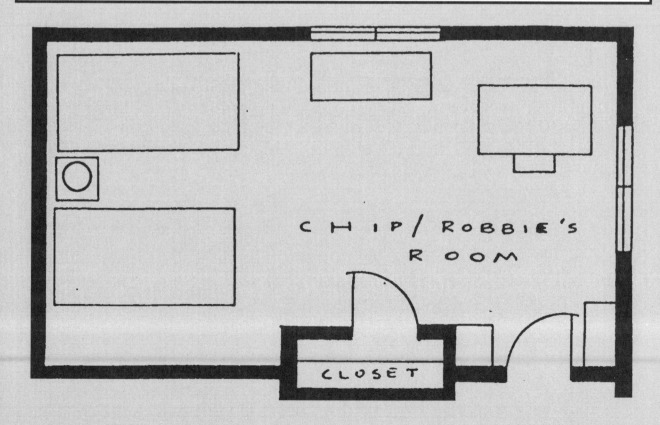

CHIP/ROBBIE'S ROOM

CLOSET

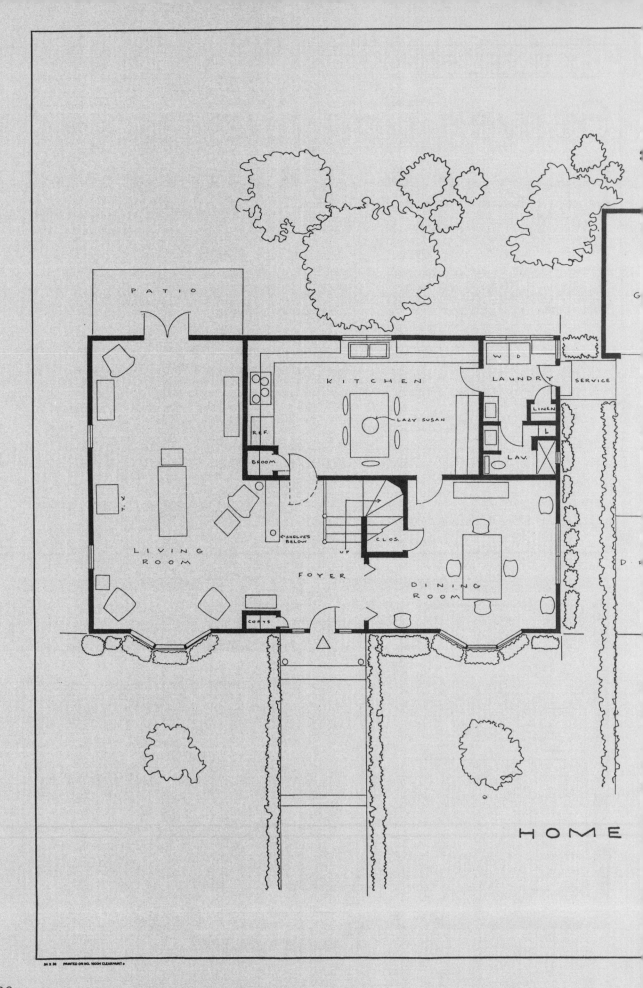

PATIO

KITCHEN

LAZY SUSAN

LAUNDRY

W D

SERVICE

LINEN

L

REF.

LAV.

BROOM

SHELVES BELOW

UP

CLOS.

LIVING ROOM

T.V.

FOYER

DINING ROOM

COATS

HOME

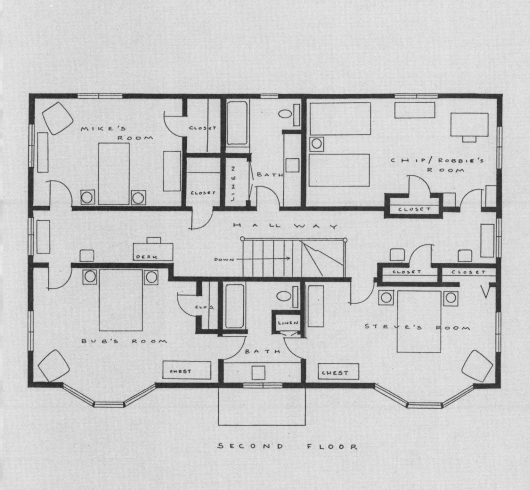

A laundry room leads to a service porch and the detached garage at the rear of the property. This is where Steve parks his latest in a series of Pontiac automobiles.

Upstairs, a central hallway leads to four bedrooms, two bathrooms and a dormitory-style telephone at the end of the hall. Animals, like their dog, Tramp, used to have free rein of the Douglas house, until a full-grown lion was found wandering the upstairs hallway. Then Steve had to put his foot down. From then on, air freshener—every day.

KITCHEN

LAZY SUSAN

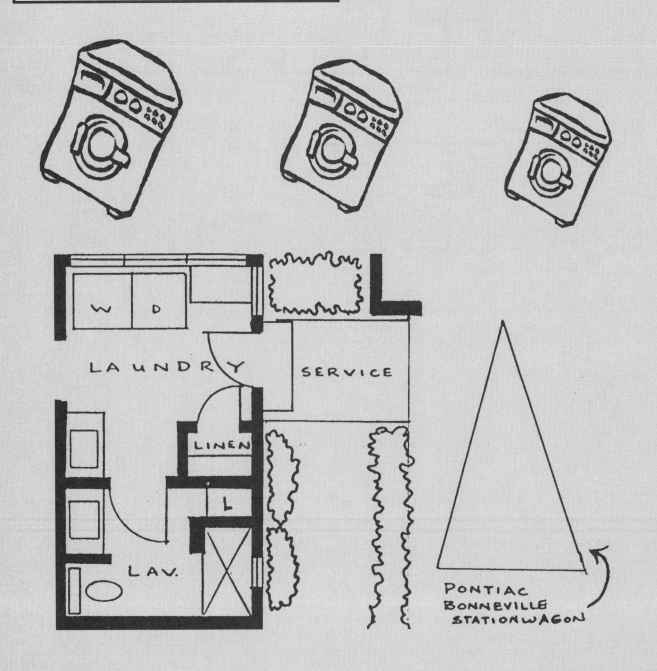

W D

LAUNDRY   SERVICE

LINEN

L

LAV.

PONTIAC BONNEVILLE STATIONWAGON

"MY THREE SONS"

Steven Douglas North Hollywood Home

The Douglas house, a rambling two-story Dutch Colonial, has the look of a Hansel-and-Gretel cottage, but on a grand, San-Fernando-Valley scale. With wood-shingle roof tiles and a motor court with enough parking for four late-model Pontiac automobiles, the home of Steve and Barbara Douglas is perfect for the aerospace engineer recently relocated to Los Angeles. With his new bride Barbara and new stepdaughter Dodie, Steve has done an excellent job of meshing his new family with his old family: Robbie, Chip and Ernie and, of course, Uncle Charlie.

The house has a narrow front yard enclosed by a picket fence. There are flower boxes, a Dutch door, a generous use of stonework. Inside, a foyer separates the open living/dining area by a waist-high bookshelf. A three-cushion suede couch faces an inviting fireplace with flanking book-shelves. French doors open out onto a patio. Sorry, though—no pool.

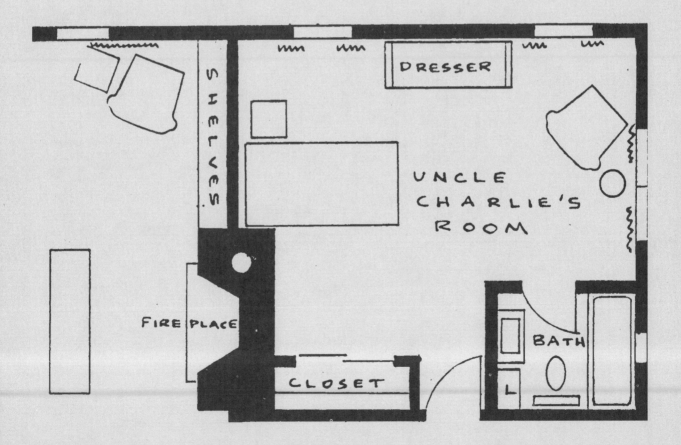

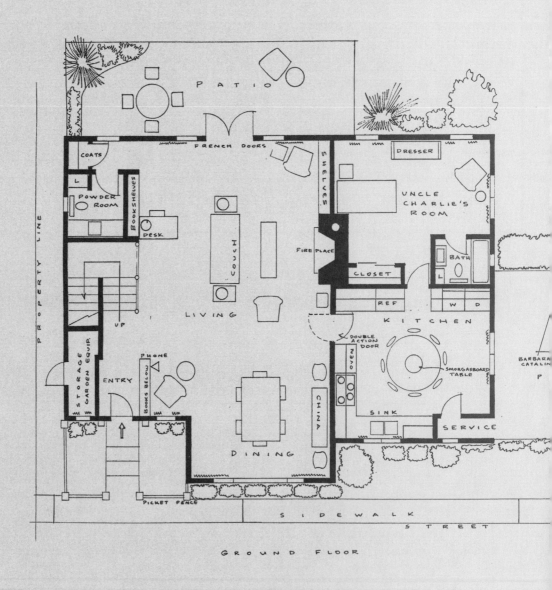

PATIO

COATS

L

POWDER ROOM

BOOKSHELVES

DESK

FRENCH DOORS

SHELVES

DRESSER

UNCLE CHARLIE'S ROOM

FIRE PLACE

COUCH

CLOSET

BATH

L

PROPERTY LINE

UP

LIVING

REF

W D

KITCHEN

STORAGE GARDEN EQUIP.

ENTRY

PHONE

BOOKS BELOW

DOUBLE ACTION DOOR

OVEN

SMORGASBOARD TABLE

BARBARA CATALINA

P

CHINA

SINK

SERVICE

DINING

PICKET FENCE

S I D E W A L K

S T R E E T

G R O U N D   F L O O R

H O I

24 X 36   PRINTED ON NO. 1000H CLEARPRINT ®

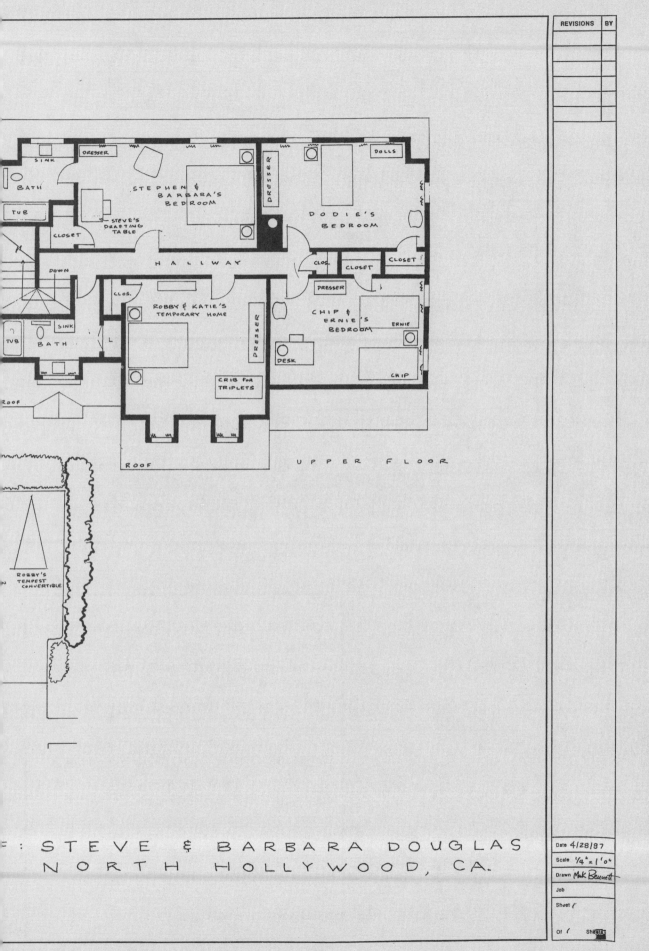

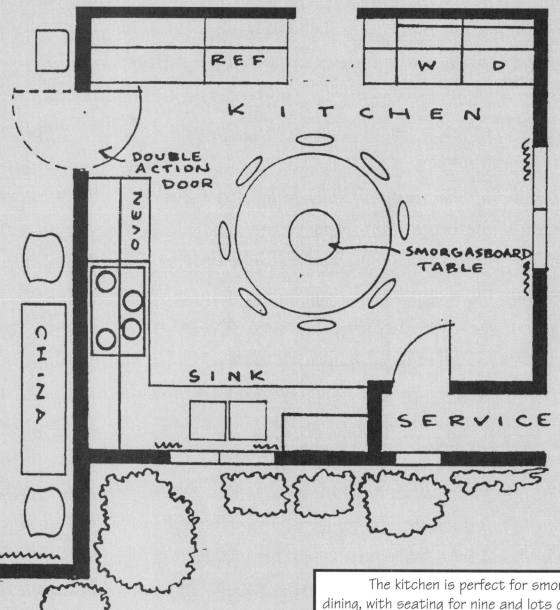

KITCHEN

REF

W D

DOUBLE
ACTION
DOOR

OVEN

CHINA

SMORGASBOARD
TABLE

SINK

SERVICE

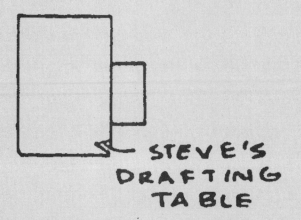

STEVE'S
DRAFTING
TABLE

The kitchen is perfect for smorgasbord dining, with seating for nine and lots of counter space for preparing large, ranch-hand meals. There are maids' quarters off the kitchen, and a mud room. Cars in the motor court are left unprotected from the sun.

Upstairs, there are bedrooms for Barbara and Steve, Dodie, Chip and Ernie, and for Robbie and Katie, and new triplets Charlie, Robbie, Jr. and Steve. Eventually Chip gets married to Polly and moves into an apartment, as do Robbie and Katie, but the extended family loves to come for visits and have dinner. Let's just hope when the dust settles and some space opens up, Steve can get his drawing-board out of his bedroom.

"MY THREE SONS"

"GIDGET"

Home of Frances "Gidget" Lawrence

Talk about a comfortable pad. This two-story rancher in the Pacific Palisades section of Los Angeles is home to the city's perkiest coed, Frances "Gidget" Lawrence, and her English-professor father.

With an open living room showcasing a stairway and an inconsequential view of the Pacific Ocean from behind French doors, the Lawrence home is done in tasteful hues of beige, rust and green. A brass chandelier hangs above the foyer. A book-lined den for Professor Lawrence is just beyond the staircase.

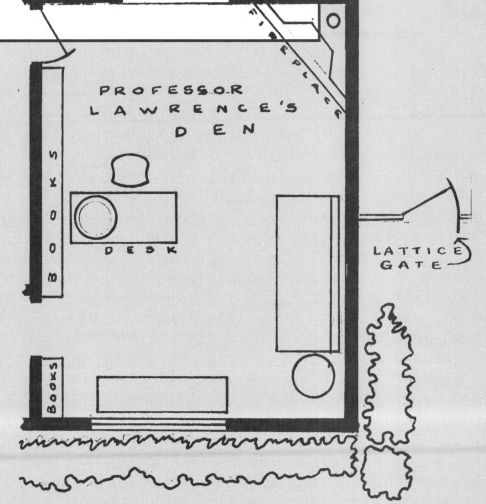

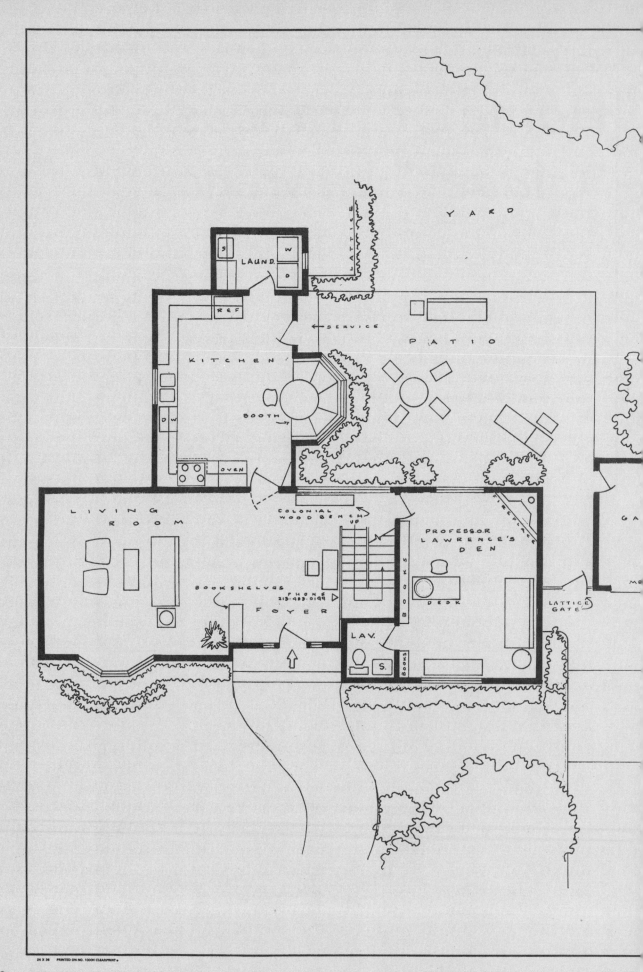

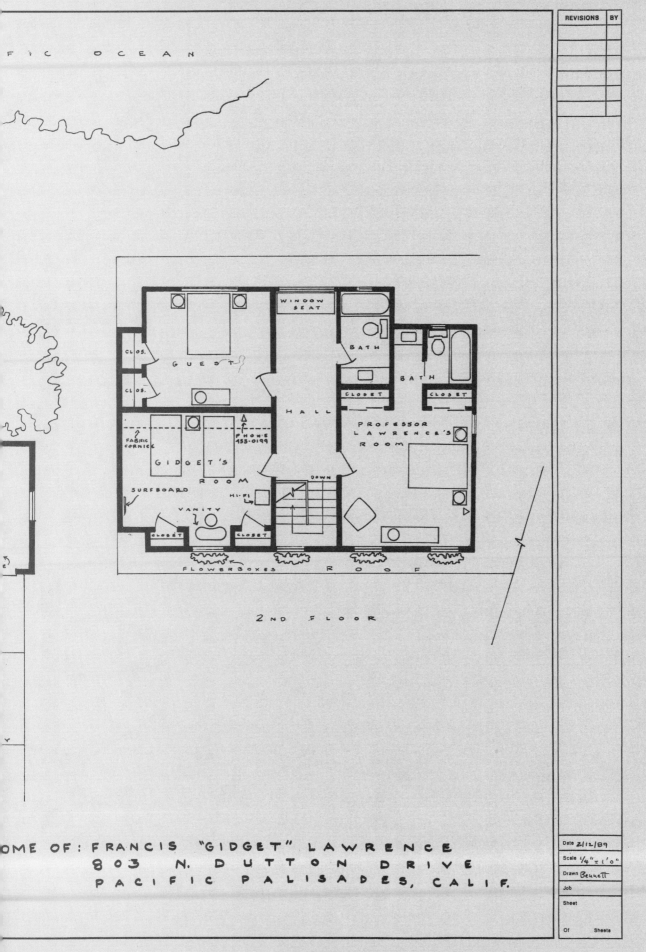

F I C   O C E A N

WINDOW
SEAT

BATH

BATH

CLOS.

CLOS.

GUEST

CLOSET

CLOSET

HALL

PROFESSOR
LAWRENCE'S
ROOM

FABRIC
CORNICE

PHONE
458-0199

GIDGET'S
ROOM

SURFBOARD

HI-FI

DOWN

VANITY

CLOSET

CLOSET

FLOWERBOXES

R O O F

2 ND   F L O O R

REVISIONS | BY

Date 2/12/89
Scale 1/4" = 1'0"
Drawn Bennett
Job
Sheet
Of   Sheets

OME OF: F R A N C I S   "G I D G E T"   L A W R E N C E
8 0 3   N.   D U T T O N   D R I V E
P A C I F I C   P A L I S A D E S,   C A L I F.

Upstairs, there are three bedrooms—one for Dad, a guest room for Gidget's sister who got married, and, of course, Gidget's room. It is decorated in pink with ruffled bedspreads. There are cozy bookshelves, a hi-fi, haircurlers, and a constantly ringing Princess telephone.

How wonderful it is to be popular. With gabfests with LaRue or Treasure, or her boyfriend Jeff Matthews aka Moondoggie, Gidget rarely has time for homework. With the Pacific Ocean just blocks away and a steady stream of late-model sportscars cruisin' down Dutton Street, what more could you expect a girl to say but, "Toodles."

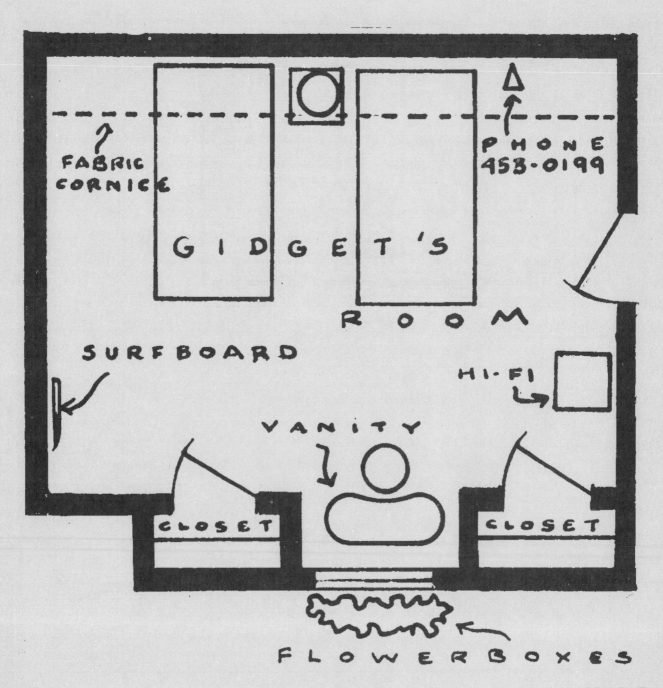

FABRIC CORNICE

PHONE 453-0199

GIDGET'S ROOM

SURFBOARD

HI-FI

VANITY

CLOSET

CLOSET

FLOWER BOXES

Home of Porter Ricks

If you are ever visiting the Everglades, a **must** stop would be the home of Porter Ricks and his sons, Bud and Sandy. Situated on a wildlife preserve just outside Miami and nestled among tall palm trees is a two-bedroom bungalow—a cottage, really—with a porch running along the facade.

There is aquatic-friendly furniture, sturdy and unassuming, inside, with an open kitchen separated by a countertop near the front door. As Porter Ricks is employed to protect and serve the natural setting, there is a state-appointed ham radio as well as a Ford station wagon out front. Two small bedrooms and a bath are at the back of the residence. The closets hold just your basic summer fashions: tank-tops, cut-offs and swimwear for the boys, and the regulation uniform for Dad. Remember, most of the living is done outdoors.

Across the road that circles the house, you have an unobstructed view of the inlet, complete with dock and ladder. There are all kinds of aquatic toys, from a low-end rowboat to a high-speed cruiser. Boogie boards, rafts, a cute little dolphin named Flipper to swim with—who would want to stay inside?

Working shutters grace the windows and doors, appropriate for protection in the event of a tropical storm, which rarely occurs. There are radios and walkie-talkies to help apprehend pesky poachers, and a complete set of scuba equipment stored inside the house.

If you are looking for a water world, this is the place to be. Just bring a towel.

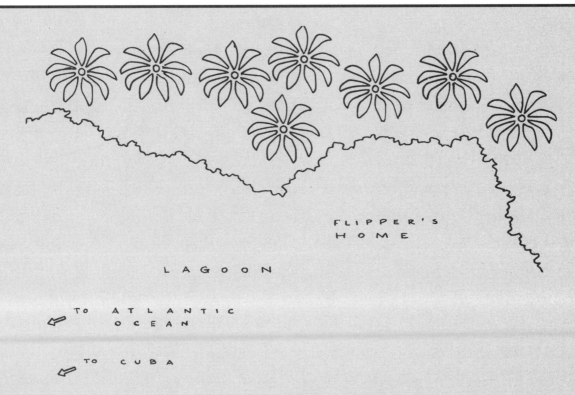

FLIPPER'S HOME

LAGOON

TO ATLANTIC OCEAN

TO CUBA

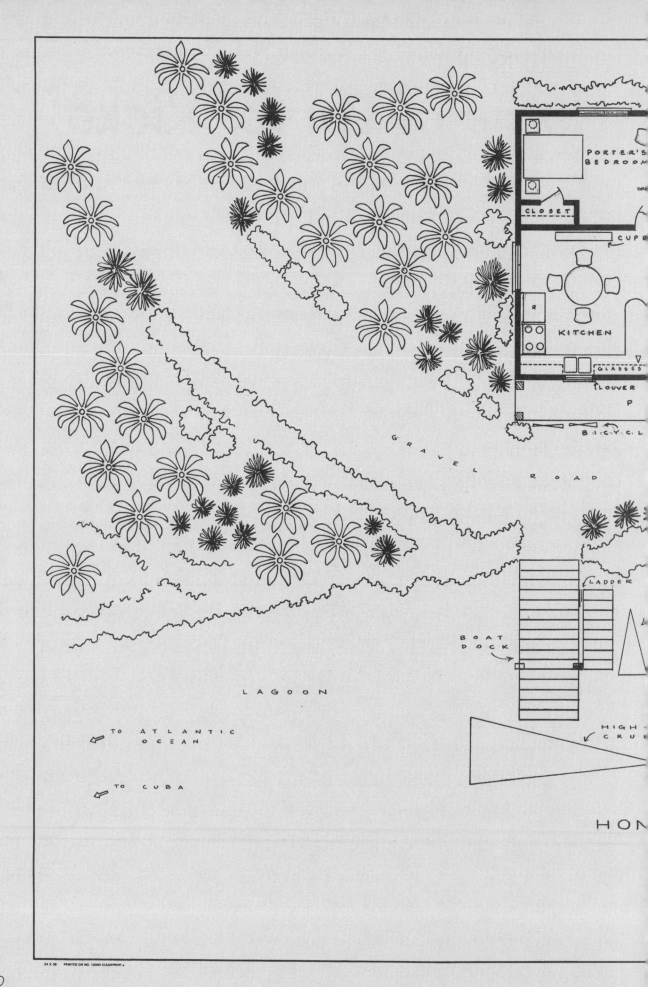

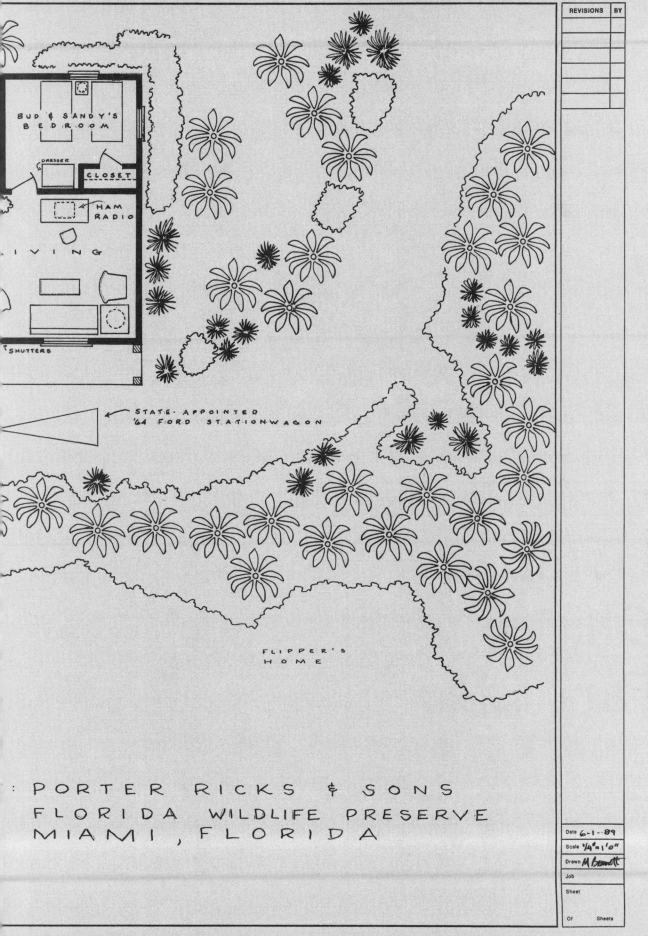

BUD & SANDY'S
B E D R O O M

DRESSER

CLOSET

HAM
RADIO

L I V I N G

SHUTTERS

STATE-APPOINTED
'64 FORD STATIONWAGON

FLIPPER'S
HOME

: P O R T E R   R I C K S   &   S O N S
F L O R I D A   W I L D L I F E   P R E S E R V E
M I A M I ,   F L O R I D A

Date 6-1--89
Scale 1/4"=1'0"
Drawn M Bennett
Job
Sheet
Of   Sheets

"FLIPPER"

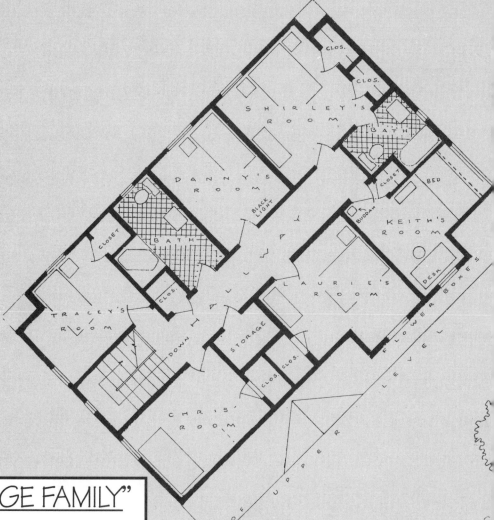

The floor plan includes the following room labels: CLOS., CLOS., SHIRLEY'S ROOM, BATH, BED, CLOSET, DANNY'S ROOM, BLACK LIGHT, BUDDAH, KEITH'S ROOM, CLOSET, BATH, HALLWAY, DESK, CLOS., LAURIE'S ROOM, FLOWER BOXES, TRACEY'S ROOM, DOWN, STORAGE, CLOS. CLOS., CHRIS'S ROOM, ROOF, UPPER LEVEL

"THE PARTRIDGE FAMILY"

Home of Shirley Partridge

On a quaint street in San Pueblo, California, is the two-story, white-sided, traditional home of Shirley Partridge and her five children. For a family that is on the road performing as a musical group, the Partridges still manage to keep their home an immaculate addition to the neighborhood. From the fresh coat of paint on the picket fence, to the

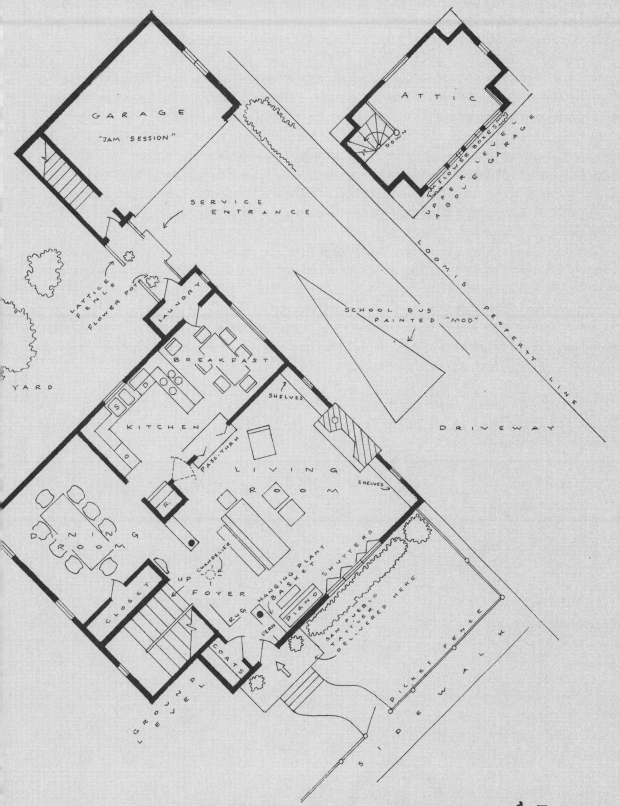

GARAGE

"JAM SESSION"

ATTIC

DOWN

FLOWER BOXES
UPPER LEVEL
ABOVE GARAGE

SERVICE
ENTRANCE

LOOMIS PROPERTY LINE

LATTICE
FENCE

FLOWER POTS

LAUNDRY

SCHOOL BUS
PAINTED "MOD"

YARD

BREAKFAST

SHELVES

KITCHEN

DRIVEWAY

PASS-THRU

LIVING

ROOM

SHELVES

DINING
ROOM

CHANDELIER

HANGING PLANT
BASKET

PIANO

SHUTTERS

CLOSET

UP

FOYER

RUG

FERN

SAN PUEBLO
TATTLER
DELIVERED HERE

PICKET FENCE

COATS

GROUND FL

SIDE WALK

E OF: SHIRLEY PARTRIDGE & FAMILY
SAN PUEBLO, CALIFORNIA

blooming flower boxes beneath the gabled windows upstairs, this home is a study in dedication and pride. The Partridge Family write their own songs, they perform, they coordinate their own stage outfits, they cut the grass, and they go to school. A marvel in time management.

Inside, we find a comfortable living area featuring area rugs over hardwood floors. There are hanging ferns from leather-strapped terra cotta pots, a three-cushioned couch, parsons tables, a bentwood rocker, and a baby grand piano for working on musical arrangements.

A formal dining room is just beyond the carpeted staircase with seating for nine. There is a roomy kitchen with all the modern conveniences such as a built-in dishwasher and refrigerator. A breakfast-nook table is where afternoon snacks occur. There is a Dutch-door service entrance at the rear of the kitchen complete with a lattice-screened breezeway connecting to the double, detached garage (with gabled, flower-boxed, windowed room above) to the main house. The garage acts as a makeshift recording studio or a place for practice sessions. All their music is melodic and pleasant. Even Mr. Loomis next door likes the noise, and often hires Keith to cut his grass.

Upstairs, each family member has a bedroom, decorated in its own individual style. Keith has a Buddha figurine prominently by the door to his room, Danny has black-light posters, Chris and Tracey have toy collections and percussion practice kits. There are two bathrooms, the main lavatory complete with a distinctive round tub.

Rubin Kincaid, their manager and family friend, likes to park his late model Chevrolet at the curb. No need to call to see if the Partridge Family is back from a road tour. Just look for the mod school bus parked in the driveway.

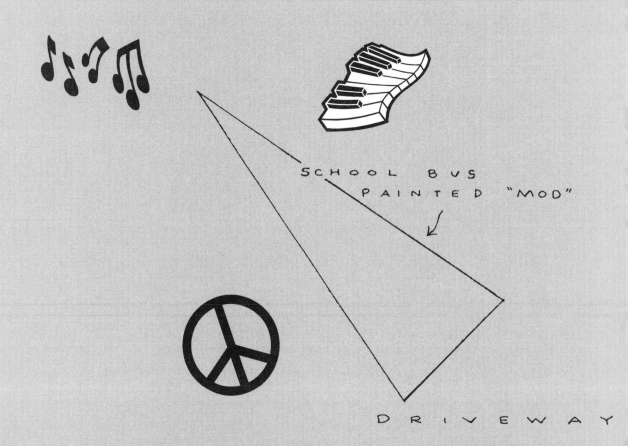

SCHOOL BUS
PAINTED "MOD"

DRIVEWAY

"THE PARTRIDGE FAMILY"

Home of Mary Richards

Okay, so it's only a studio, but what a great apartment. On the second floor of a converted Victorian, Miss Richards enjoys a breathtaking view of Minneapolis from her balcony, a cozy kitchen with under-the-counter refrigerator. and a step-down living area. All right, the heating from the stove-pipe in the used brick corner is faulty, and the air vent by the front door is less than eavesdrop-proof, but Apartment D makes up for it all in charm.

A roll-down stained-glass partition closes off the kitchen, a separate dressing area with a bath hides a new spring wardrobe, and the 14-foot exposed beam ceilings are breathtaking. Heavy use of crown moldings and wall sconces add extra ambience. Furnishings are "working girl" but chic. All the common areas such as hallways and stairwells are carpeted.

Even though Mary's apartment has been burglarized, one feels that the mailboxes in the downstairs hallway are polished brass and that there is an enclosed garage for Mary's pampered Mustang. All in all, not a bad neighborhood—and, according to Mary's boss, Mr. Grant, one with some of the best saloons in town.

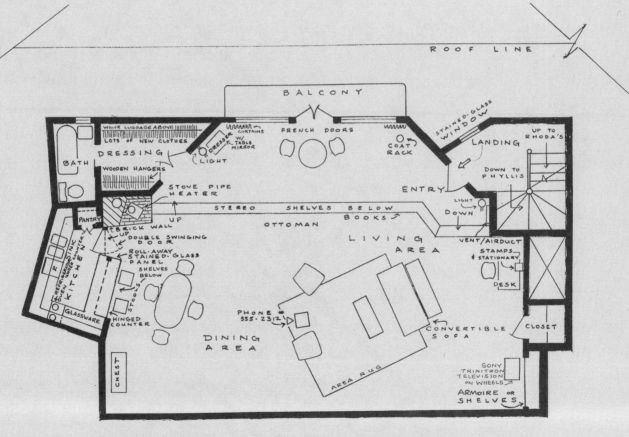

HOME OF: MARY RICHARDS
119 NORTH WEATHERLY
APT. D
MINNEAPOLIS, MINNESOTA

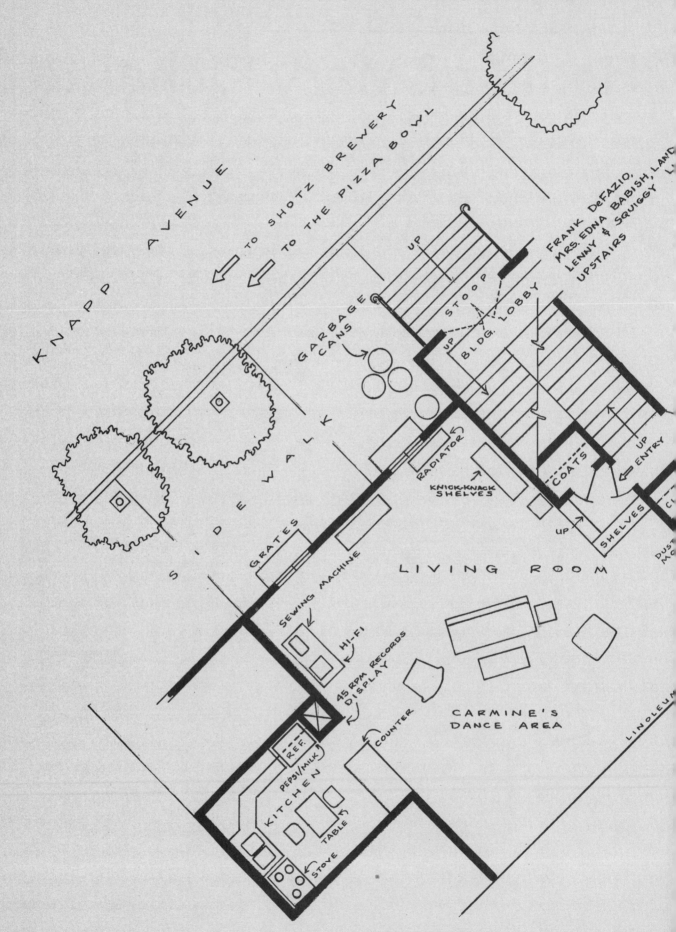

KNAPP AVENUE

TO SHOTZ BREWERY

TO THE PIZZA BOWL

SIDEWALK

GRATES

GARBAGE CANS

UP

STOOP

UP

BLDG. LOBBY

FRANK DeFAZIO,
MRS. EDNA BABISH, LAND
LENNY & SQUIGGY L
UPSTAIRS

RADIATOR

KNICK-KNACK
SHELVES

COATS

UP ENTRY

SHELVES

UP

DUST
MO

LIVING ROOM

SEWING MACHINE

HI-FI

45 RPM RECORDS
DISPLAY

COUNTER

CARMINE'S
DANCE AREA

LINOLEUM

REF.

PEPSI/MILK

KITCHEN

TABLE

STOVE

"LAVERNEAND SHIRLEY"

Laverne DeFazio & Shirley Finney

Deep in the heart of Milwaukee, in the basement of an apartment building on Knapp Avenue, is the home of Laverne DeFazio and Shirley Finney. Step down into the large linoleum-floored living room. Sturdy, discount-house furniture is arranged in a sparse way. A small kitchen is off in an alcove and large enough to house a kitchen table and chairs. Forty-five RPM records grace the walls and probably hide some flaw in the light floral wallpaper.

A set of windows flank a faulty radiator and is perfect for checking out the latest in fashion footwear on the passersby strolling on the sidewalk above. A sewing machine, bulletin board, high-school pennants, stuffed animals: this apartment is not for the sophisticated. It's basic, low-end, a little rough & tumble. So what if Carmine does an elaborate dance move off the couch, or if Lenny spills a beer on the furniture. No sweat. There's nothing in this room that cannot be replaced.

BASEMENT LEVEL

HAMPER

CLOSET

BEDROOM

SHIRLEY'S
STUFFED ANIMAL
"BOO BOO KITTY"

DRESSER

TWIN BEDS

LAVERNE'S
SWEATERS
WITH "L"

HOME OF: LAVERNE DeFAZIO & SHIRLEY FINNEY
730 KNAPP AVENUE
MILWAUKEE, WISCONSIN

There is one bedroom with two twin beds and a single bath with matching tile and fixture colors. Of course, the real appeal of this abode is its close proximity to the Pizza Bowl and Shotz Brewery. And there is two-hour parking at the curb.

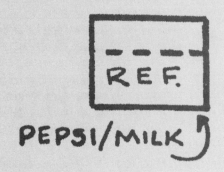

PEPSI/MILK

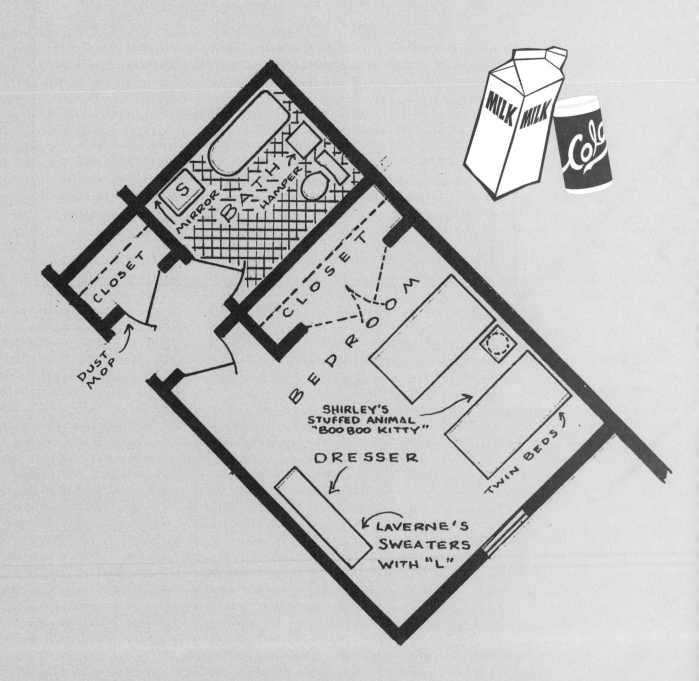

CLOSET

DUST MOP

MIRROR

BATH

HAMPER

CLOSET

BEDROOM

SHIRLEY'S STUFFED ANIMAL "BOO BOO KITTY"

DRESSER

TWIN BEDS

LAVERNE'S SWEATERS WITH "L"

"LOST IN SPACE"

Home of Professor John Robinson and Crew

What a great house! Brushed aluminum exterior, lots of glass, automated entrances. All in the round and on two levels. Comes with all those toys for space exploration. GREAT for extended family living situations, and can transport you to faraway places like Jupiter or Mars. Can even transcend time travel. Complete automation—from food preparation to wardrobe changes. Comes with easy-to-sass Robot and self-stored landcruiser bus with seating for six.

Now if this is the wave of the future, how do you buy one? Do you have to register your house with the DMV?

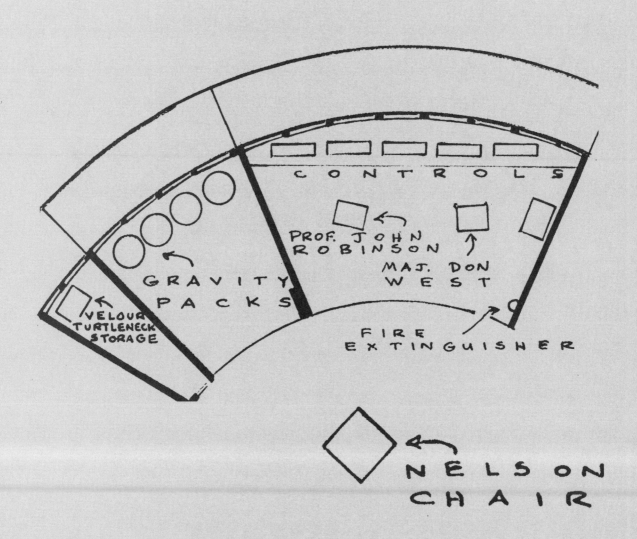

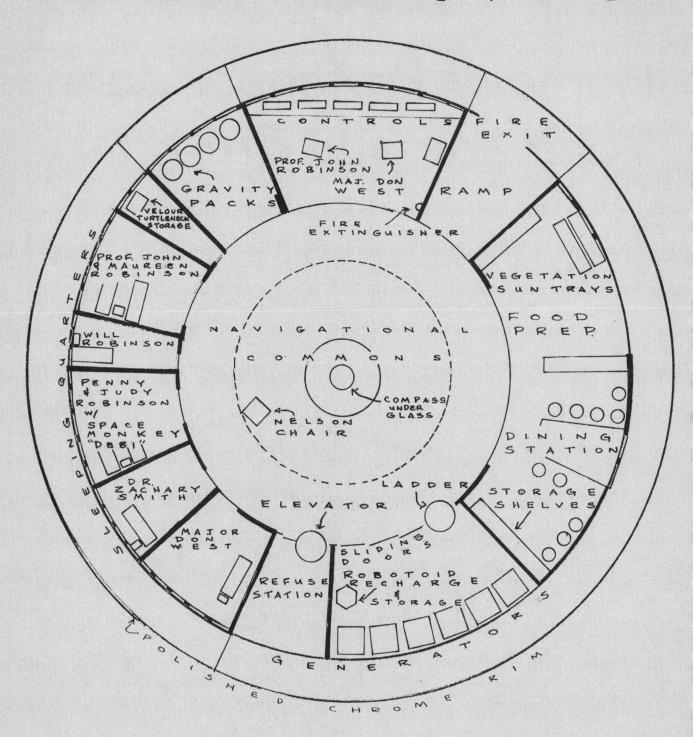

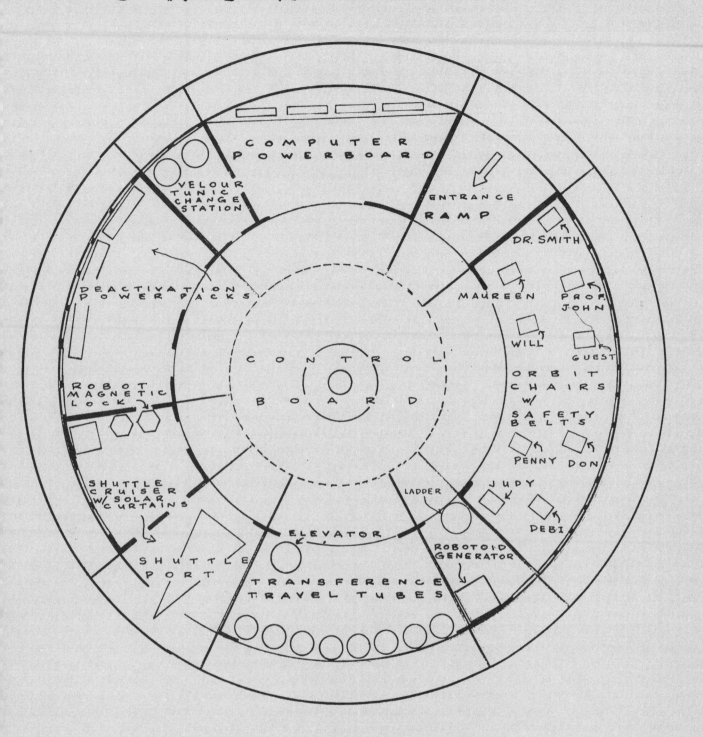

THE JUPITER II
HOME OF: PROF. JOHN ROBINSON & FAMILY
MAJOR DON WEST
DR. ZACHARY SMITH

THE GALAXY

"GILLIGAN'S ISLAND"

Gilligan's Island

In the middle of the Pacific Ocean is an island inhabited by five mainland tourists along with a sea-worthy skipper and his entire crew—Gilligan. They have been marooned here since a tropical storm tossed ashore their petite "S.S. Minnow" during a three-hour tour off the coast of Honolulu.

They've done the best they could, building a quaint, Polynesian-theme quadrangle of five huts, each with its own distinctive look. Jonas Grumby, the Skipper, and his helpmate Gilligan have utilitarian digs with double hammocks. Ginger and Mary Ann have a more bachelorette hut, with a make-up table and a makeshift armoire for slinky dresses. The Professor has a laboratory and simple cot. Thurston and Lovie Howell have French doors and twin beds.

There is an electricity-making stationary bike (for charging batteries), a pedal car made of bamboo that Gilligan drives. lounge chairs for sunbathing by the lagoon, a stage on which to satisfy Thespian urges, and a central dining table with benches for communal meals. Tiki torches give an elegant glow to night-time activities.

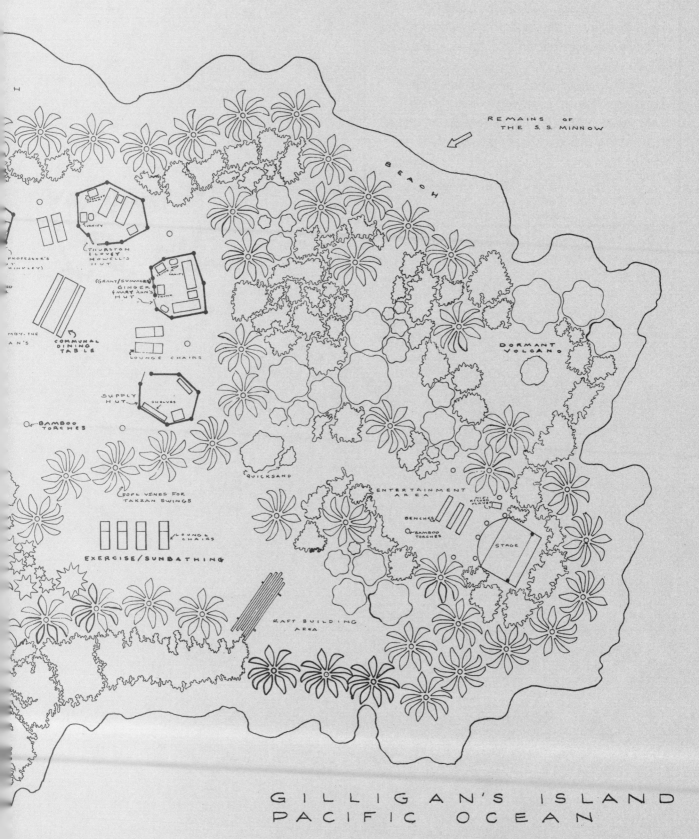

REMAINS OF
THE S.S. MINNOW

BEACH

PROFESSOR'S
(ROY HINKLEY)

THURSTON
(LOVEY HOWELL'S
HUT)

(GRANT/SUMMERS
GINGER
& MARY ANN'S
HUT)

GILLIGAN'S
HUT

COMMUNAL
DINING
TABLE

LOUNGE CHAIRS

SUPPLY
HUT

SHELVES

BAMBOO
TORCHES

QUICKSAND

DORMANT
VOLCANO

ROPE VINES FOR
TARZAN SWINGS

ENTERTAINMENT
AREA

BENCHES

BAMBOO
TORCHES

STAGE

LOUNGE
CHAIRS

EXERCISE/SUNBATHING

RAFT BUILDING
AREA

GILLIGAN'S ISLAND
PACIFIC OCEAN

There are enough natural wonders and World War II booby traps to keep any visitor occupied.

A main activity is raft building down by the lagoon, a pastime that never seems to get off the ground, or out to sea, for that matter.

A positively tropical paradise, this island, invisible on most maps, could make a great resort. The Howells have enough clothes to dress any cocktail party guest, and if one were to pick a hut to vacation in, the perfect choice would be Skipper and Gilligan's digs. They've got the radio.

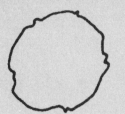

DORMANT VOLCANO

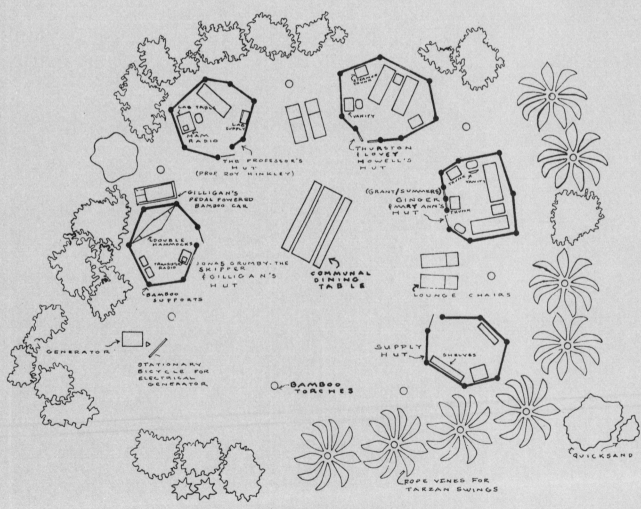

INCOMING
WOUNDED

HELICOPTER
PAD

M * A * S * H
Compound

Let's say you're wounded, God forbid, in the war effort, and you are shipped via helicopter to a Mobile Amy Surgical Hospital deep in the confines of Korea.

You are transported on a canvas stretcher down a path from the heliport to a bunch of tents, an olive-drab slum, a makeshift government-issue village with bedpans worked into a center-of-town water-sculpture.

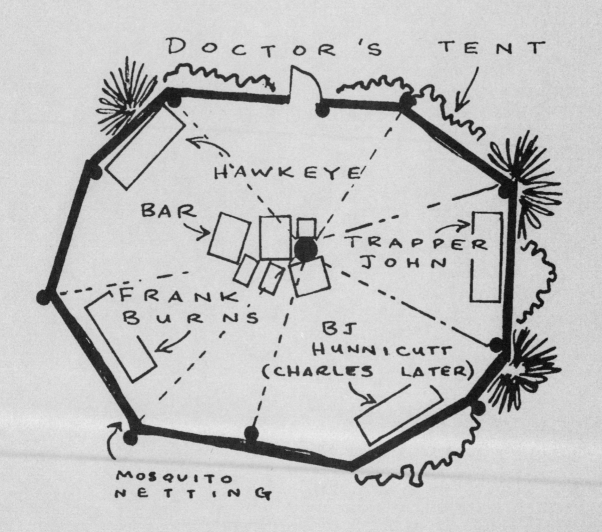

DOCTOR'S TENT

HAWKEYE

BAR

TRAPPER JOHN

FRANK BURNS

BJ HUNNICUTT (CHARLES LATER)

MOSQUITO NETTING

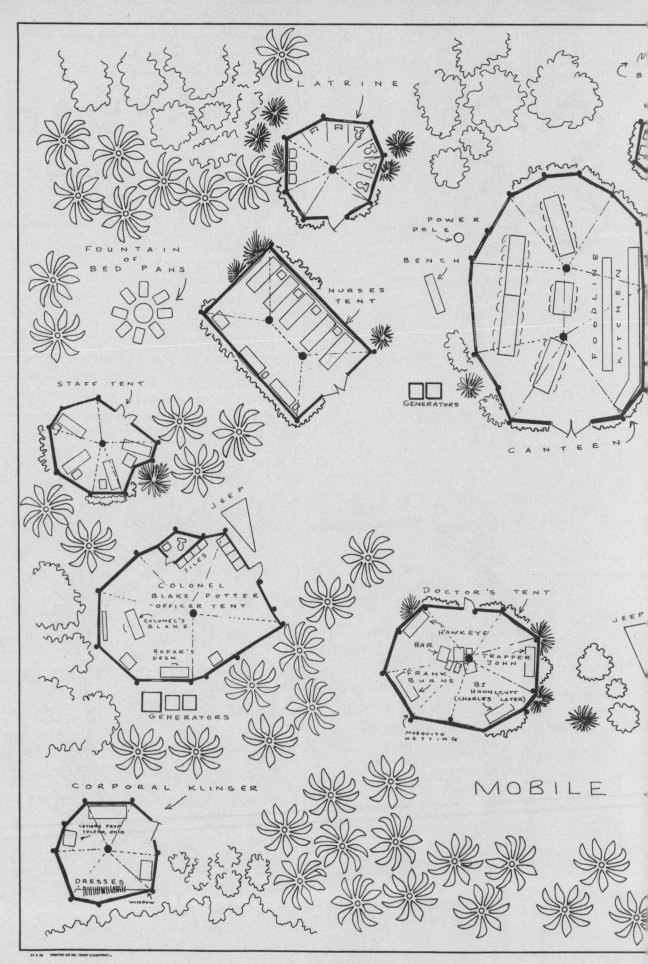

LATRINE

FOUNTAIN
of
BED PANS

NURSES
TENT

POWER
POLE

BENCH

GENERATORS

FOODLINE
KITCHEN

CANTEEN

STAFF TENT

JEEP

FILES

COLONEL
BLAKE / POTTER
OFFICER TENT

COLONEL'S
BLAKE

RADAR'S
DESK

GENERATORS

DOCTOR'S TENT

HAWKEYE

BAR

TRAPPER
JOHN

FRANK
BURNS

BJ
HUNNICUTT
(CHARLES LATER)

MOSQUITO
NETTING

JEEP

CORPORAL KLINGER

LETTERS FROM
TOLEDO, OHIO

DRESSES

WINDOW

MOBILE

24 X 36   PRINTED ON NO. 1000H CLEARPRINT

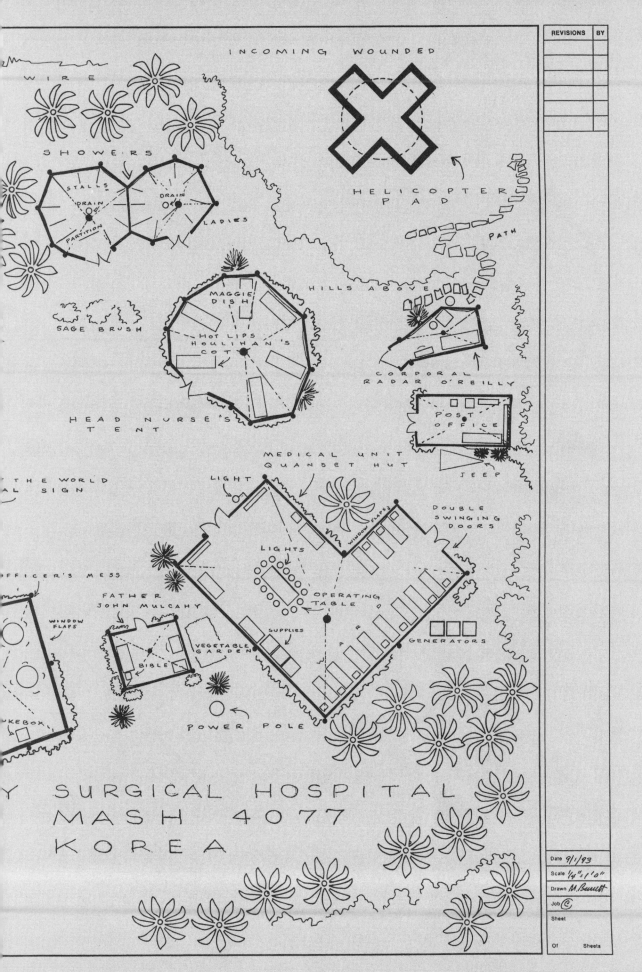

INCOMING WOUNDED

WIRE

SHOWERS

STALLS
DRAIN
PARTITION
DRAIN
LADIES

HELICOPTER
PAD

PATH

HILLS ABOVE

SAGE BRUSH

MAGGIE
DISH

Hot LIPS
HOULIHAN'S
COT

CORPORAL
RADAR O'REILLY

POST
OFFICE

HEAD NURSE'S
TENT

JEEP

THE WORLD
L SIGN

MEDICAL UNIT
QUANSET HUT

LIGHT

DOUBLE
SWINGING
DOORS

WINDOW FLAPS

LIGHTS

OFFICER'S MESS

FATHER
JOHN MULCAHY

WINDOW
FLAPS

OPERATING
TABLE

VEGETABLE
GARDEN

SUPPLIES

GENERATORS

BIBLE

KEBOX

POWER POLE

Y SURGICAL HOSPITAL
MASH 4077
KOREA

Date 9/1/93
Scale 1/4"=1'0"
Drawn M.Burnett
Job C
Sheet
Of   Sheets

"M*A*S*H"

127

They wheel you into surgery, housed in a large tent, with portable klieg lights hovering above you. Your doctor has martinis on his breath and the attending nurse is flirting with you. There is music from the canteen and there is laughter and the sound of people dancing. A man in a dress with matching high heels saunters past—and it's not even dusk yet. Someone injects you with a sedative, and as you nod off, you don't feel so bad about tripping over that barbed wire on your reconnaissance mission.

If you've got to be in a war, this is the place to be.

CORPORAL KLINGER

LETTERS FROM TOLEDO, OHIO

DRESSES

WINDOW

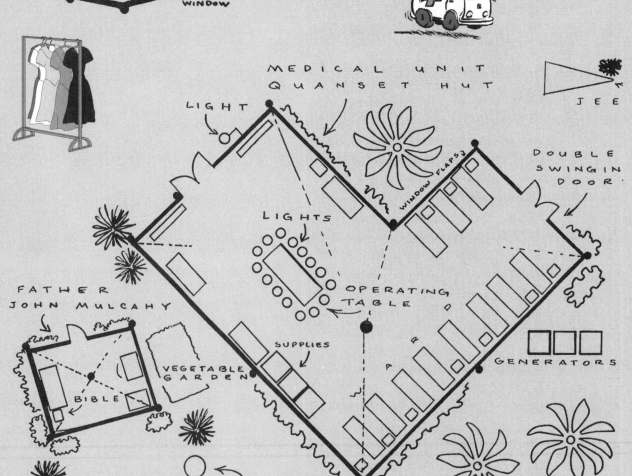

MEDICAL UNIT QUANSET HUT

JEE

LIGHT

DOUBLE SWINGIN DOOR

WINDOW FLAPS

LIGHTS

OPERATING TABLE

FATHER JOHN MULCAHY

BIBLE

VEGETABLE GARDEN

SUPPLIES

GENERATORS

POWER POLE

"PERRY MASON"

Office of Perry Mason

When you are the most celebrated attorney in Los Angeles, you can afford a posh law office on Wilshire Boulevard in the Bank of California Building.

Picture yourself being accused of murder, and strolling into the reception area of Perry Mason, Attorney at Law. To the left, modern, functional upholstered couches; to the right, Gertie, the street-wise blonde, at the switchboard.

Beyond a black-lacquered Japanese screen and potted philodendron is the desk of Perry's right hand and legal secretary, Miss Della Street. Separating the switchboard and Della's work station is a row of black filing cabinets, filled with some of the most celebrated case files in the annals of the Los Angeles justice system. On the tasteful couch with matching chair and end table, Miss Street will dry your tears, fix you a perfect cup of coffee (probably from the small service room that connects her office to the law library) and reassure you that you have come to the right place.

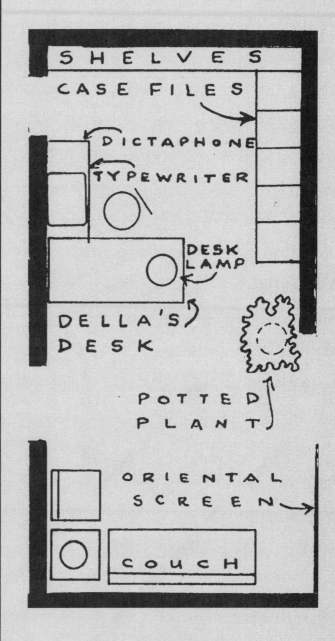

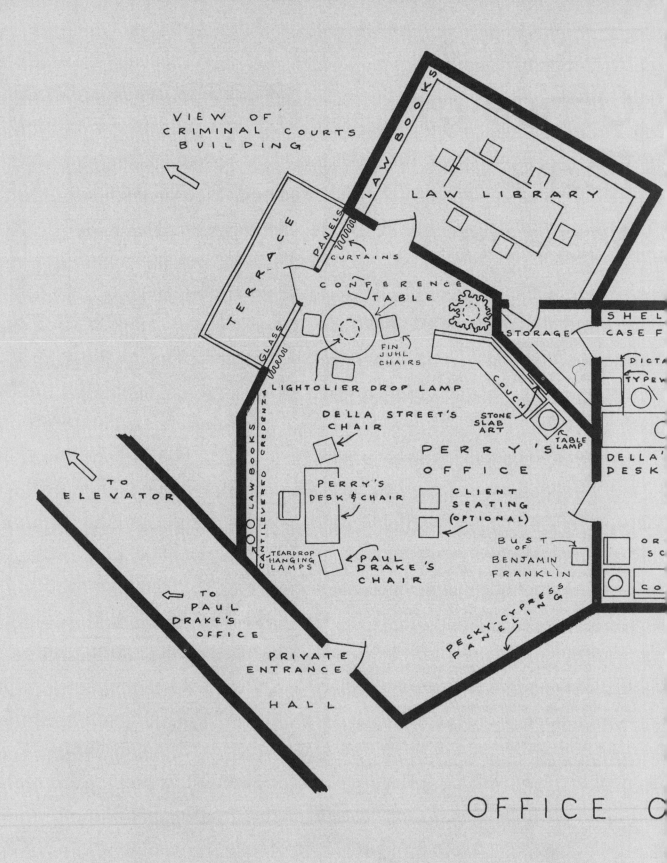

VIEW OF CRIMINAL COURTS BUILDING

LAW BOOKS

LAW LIBRARY

TERRACE

PANELS

CURTAINS

CONFERENCE TABLE

STORAGE

SHEL...

CASE F...

GLASS

FIN JUHL CHAIRS

LIGHTOLIER DROP LAMP

COUCH

DICTA...

TYPEW...

DELLA STREET'S CHAIR

STONE SLAB ART

TABLE LAMP

PERRY'S OFFICE

DELLA'... DESK

TO ELEVATOR

CANTILEVERED CREDENZA

LAW BOOKS

PERRY'S DESK & CHAIR

CLIENT SEATING (OPTIONAL)

TO PAUL DRAKE'S OFFICE

TEARDROP HANGING LAMPS

PAUL DRAKE'S CHAIR

BUST OF BENJAMIN FRANKLIN

OR... SC...

CO...

PRIVATE ENTRANCE

PECKY-CYPRESS PANELING

HALL

OFFICE C

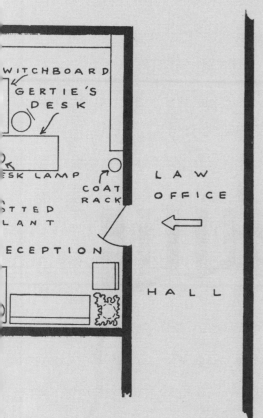

WITCHBOARD

GERTIE'S
DESK

SK LAMP

COAT
RACK

TTED
LANT

ECEPTION

LAW

OFFICE

←

HALL

At the designated appointment time, you are lead through a single four-foot mahogany door into the berber-carpeted sanctum of Mr. Mason's world—pecky-cypress paneling, an angular low-slung white couch, Finn Juhl conference table and chairs, and a floor-to-ceiling glass panel, terraced view. You realize not only has Mr. Mason hired a decorator, he's also raided the high-end Baker, Knapp & Tubbs showroom. A snooty piece of art (relief-carved stone) hangs behind the couch and a bronze sculpture rests on a pedestal by the door. A Lightolier chandelier holds court above the conference table, just before the entrance to Perry's fully-stocked law library.

Mr. Mason's desk is a sleek modern peg-boarded affair with a floating veneered top holding a simple leather fountain-pen set. Behind the desk, a credenza stands against the wall, caressing a series of books, encased between two globe-shaped bookends. Three tear-drop lamps hang from the ceiling above this unit. To the left is a secret entrance/exit door, often used by private investigator Paul Drake, who has an office down the hall.

From the posh surroundings, you suddenly realize that the cup of coffee Della just handed you may cost you more than you can afford.

ERRY MASON, ATTY.
HE BANK OF CALIFORNIA BLDG.
/ILSHIRE BLVD.
OS ANGELES, CALIFORNIA

About the Author

By day, Mark Bennett is a Beverly Hills postal worker on Wilshire Boulevard. All other times, Bennett is a young artist whose blueprints have been shown by galleries in New York, Los Angeles, Seattle, Chicago, and Cincinnati. His work has been featured on "*CNN Showbiz Today*," "*E! Entertainment News*," and "*The Mike and Maty Show*," as well as in <u>*Harper's Magazine*</u>, <u>*TV Guide*</u>, the <u>*L.A. Times*</u>, and <u>*Art Issues*</u>. He is represented by the Mark Moore Gallery in Santa Monica, California.